▶️ ADVENTUROUS PUB WALKS ◀️
IN
SOMERSET

ADVENTUROUS PUB WALKS
IN
SOMERSET

Roger Evans

COUNTRYSIDE BOOKS
NEWBURY BERKSHIRE

First published 2007
© Roger Evans 2007

COUNTRYSIDE BOOKS
3 Catherine Road
Newbury, Berkshire

To view our complete range of books,
please visit us at
www. countrysidebooks co.uk

ISBN 978 1 84674 032 9

Cover picture shows a view of
Glastonbury Tor from
the River Brue, taken
by Bill Meadows

Designed by Peter Davies, Nautilus Design

Produced through MRM Associates Ltd., Reading
Typeset by Jean Cussons Typesetting, Diss, Norfolk
Printed by Borcombe Printers plc, Romsey

CONTENTS

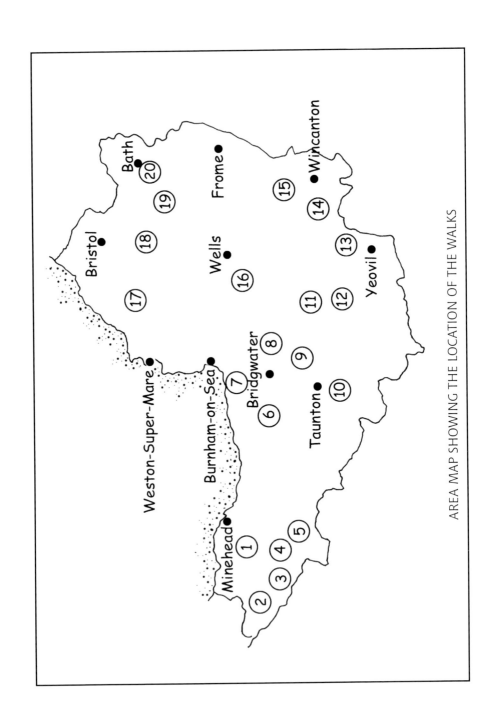

AREA MAP SHOWING THE LOCATION OF THE WALKS

PUBLISHER'S NOTE

*W*e hope that you obtain considerable enjoyment from this book; great care has been taken in its preparation. Although at the time of publication all routes followed public rights of way or permitted paths, diversion orders can be made and permissions withdrawn.

We cannot, of course, be held responsible for such diversion orders and any inaccuracies in the text which result from these or any other changes to the routes or any damage which might result from walkers trespassing on private property. We are anxious though that all details covering the walks are kept up to date and would therefore welcome information from readers which would be relevant to future editions.

The simple sketch maps that accompany the walks in this book are based on notes made by the author whilst checking out the routes on the ground. However, for the benefit of a proper map, we do recommend that you purchase the relevant Ordnance Survey sheet covering your walk. The Ordnance Survey maps are widely available, especially through booksellers and local newsagents.

INTRODUCTION

Somerset is ideally suited to the concept of *Adventurous Pub Walks*. The high ground of Mendip with its stone walls and grey-stone houses, scattered in isolation, offers extensive remote walking. At the opposite end of the county, there is Exmoor with its deep-cleft valleys and thatched-roof communities. South Somerset rejoices in rolling hills with fawn-stone villages whilst central

WRINGTON, ONE OF SOMERSET'S MANY DELIGHTFUL VILLAGES

Somerset has a varied coastline and the low-lying Levels. The walks in this book capture this great variety and take in many of the county's historic and pre-historic sites such as the battlefields of Sedgemoor and the stone circles at Stanton Drew created over 2,000 years ago, as well as providing spectacular views.

It is not only the landscape that makes Somerset so well suited to the walker. Each walk starts from, or near, a village pub, and alternative venues for refreshments are given along the route where appropriate. The pubs described have been chosen for their warmth of reception, the quality of their food and ales, and many of them for their willingness to say 'Yes, dogs are always welcome'. Buster, my Border Collie, has been my constant companion throughout these walks and hence a country pub which welcomes dogs is almost a prerequisite for me, as I know it is for so many walkers. I have even discovered pubs that deliver a dog bowl of water as part of the drinks round, and one that boasted a dogs' menu!

You may well have picked up this book wondering, 'Is this what I need? Won't adventurous walks be too difficult for me?' So let me put your mind at rest. The walks are all between 6½ and 11 miles in length, and explore every corner of the county. Some include stretches of hillside walking, such as the climb to Glastonbury Tor, while others are gentle and on the flat. At the time of writing, and at the time of walking, I am rapidly approaching 60 years of age and am at least three stones overweight. And I thoroughly enjoyed every walk and every pub that was the reward at the end.

Apart from my dog, Buster, my other frequent companion has been Gareth, my eldest son, whose company has been much appreciated, not least since I let him carry the backpack! On all of these walks, we have used the appropriate Ordnance Survey map (the relevant map number is given in the directions), and we have worn sound pairs of boots and appropriate clothing. I would advise the reader to follow the same practice. With a long walk, the enjoyment is doubled if you take your time. The walks can take anything from three hours to a full day, according to how much time you take to 'stand and stare'. English weather can change rapidly, especially on the higher ground of Mendip and Exmoor. So go well prepared, enjoy the scenery and savour the hospitality. Happy walking!

Roger Evans

EXFORD AND
THE EXE VALLEY

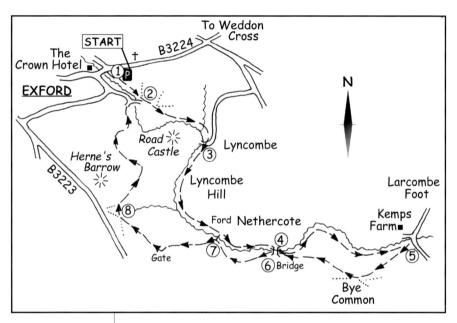

Distance:
6 or 8½ miles

Map: OS Explorer OL9 Exmoor

Starting Point:
Exford free car
park.
GR 854383

How to get there: *From the A396 between Tiverton and
Dunster, take the B3224 from Wheddon Cross, signposted
for Exford. Entering the village, the free car park can be
found by turning left just before the Crown Hotel.*

THE CROWN HOTEL, EXFORD

*E*xford is one of Exmoor's prettiest villages and is surrounded by stunning moorland scenery. This lovely walk follows the upper reaches of the River Exe, passing just a few isolated hill farms along the route. Here you can expect to see the ancient breed of Exmoor ponies and, on a good day, red deer and overhead the soaring buzzards. Watch out for the elusive dippers, black birds that swim underwater along the fast flowing stream. The outward journey follows the left bank of the river as it tumbles downstream. At Nethercote, you have the choice of extending the 6 mile walk into one of 8½ miles. The return leg heads steeply uphill from Nethercote Bridge onto Room Hill to enjoy excellent views before dropping back down into Exford. The village is an ideal centre for walking, riding or fishing on the River Exe. There is an annual horse show held here each August, Exford being the home of the Devon and Somerset Staghounds. The hunt has had its kennels here ever since 1875 and the shops which nestle around the picturesque village green reflect a community whose culture is based on hunting, fishing, shooting and riding. Across the green from the Crown Hotel is the village school, classically Victorian in style. The village also boasts a Youth Hostel, housed in another Victorian building which stands in its own grounds on the bank of the River Exe.

The Crown Hotel will be found right in the centre of the village. It is a 17th century coaching inn and sporting hotel with 3 acres of gardens alongside the River Exe. I have sat here eating lunch and watched dippers in the river doing the same. The hotel even has its own stretch of salmon fishing, as well as stabling and livery. As this is hunting territory, dogs and horses are welcome. Internally the hotel is full of character with beamed ceilings and an open log fire. The food is excellent and a wide choice is available, supported by local real ales. Accommodation is available.

Telephone: *01643 831554.*

The Walk

① Leave the car park by the gate at the far end, beyond the Exmoor National Park hut, and follow the riverbank. After two more gates you will find two field gates side-by-side. Take the kissing-gate on the right, signposted 'Footpath to **Lovers Lane**, **Highercombe** and **Lyncombe**'.

② Follow the left-hand field boundary to reach a barn. Pass through the waymarked gate to the right of the barn and follow the right-hand field boundary around one and a half sides of the field, to reach a gate and stile. Cross the stile and follow the track as it drops down into the valley. Continue ahead with the river to your right, to reach a gate marked '**Beach Pool**'.

You will see a number of these named pools along this walk. The signs indicate recognised points for salmon fishing. When the salmon are running upstream to spawn, these pools provide useful resting places for the salmon to recover their energy before the next arduous stretch up the river. The Environment Agency rules for fishing these waters can be incredibly complicated: for example, 'After 16th August, salmon of 27½" or over (8 pounds) to be returned unless injured, in which event, the next salmon caught under size limit to be returned. Red or coloured fish to be returned, no fishing by prawn or shrimp in September'.

Continue along the riverbank, crossing three stiles before entering a marshy field. Yellow waymarkers indicate a dry route through this area. On reaching a farm lane, pass through the farm and continue straight ahead to reach the end of the lane.

③ Enter the field and keep straight ahead, following the obvious track that leads you around **Lyncombe Hill** on your left. Eventually the track becomes a lane. Watch out for a gate on your right-hand side, which has a notice referring to the path to **Nethercote Bridge**. Turn right here through the gate and drop down towards the river, bearing left to follow the riverbank to reach a stoned track at **Nethercote Bridge**.

At point 4, the shorter walk continues by passing through the gate immediately across the bridge and then following the directions from point 6.

④ Cross the bridge and turn left to follow the farm road all the way to the metalled road and bridge at **Larcombe Foot**.

This river walk offers good opportunities for spotting dippers and kingfishers. At Larcombe Foot you may see boxes hanging in the trees. These are delivery boxes for the local tradesmen delivering to the remote farms.

⑤ A few yards before **Larcombe bridge**, turn right to head up a track which runs back above the road you have just walked. Follow this uphill onto **Bye Common**, heading for the right-hand end of a stone wall. Turn right at the wall and follow the fence between the brackened moorland and the grassland. On reaching a waymarked gate, pass through and then turn left to follow the track down to **Nethercote Bridge**, which you crossed on your outward journey.

⑥ Immediately before the bridge, turn left through the waymarked gate marked as the 'Path to **Room Hill**'. With the river on your right-hand side, follow the riverbank, pass through a gate and stream and continue straight ahead until you reach a gate by a ford across the **River Exe**.

⑦ Pass through the gate and continue ahead with the river bank on your right. In a short distance, turn left to go up a stony track alongside a small brook. This leads you steeply up onto **Room Hill**. On reaching the open moorland, continue straight ahead towards the brow of the hill. When you come to a gate in the left-hand field boundary, turn right onto the path that leads away from the gate through the scattered hawthorn trees and across the head of a combe to a convergence of paths.

⑧ Bear right, signposted **Exford**, keeping to the wide track, which eventually runs parallel to a field boundary on your left-hand side. On reaching a tree-lined hedgerow, keep straight ahead, through the field gate

BUSTER DRINKS FROM THE RIVER EXE, POINT 6 ON THE WALK

and follow the left-hand field boundary to the next gate following the blue arrow. Continue ahead through the gate and again along the left-hand field boundary. The track ends at a gate on your left. Pass through the gate to descend a narrow track. Cross the stream and continue straight ahead on the same track.

Go through the next gate and keep going down to a metalled road. Turn right and right again at **Court Farm** to cross the river. Turn left and retrace your steps to the car park.

Date walk completed:

SIMONSBATH AND THE RIVER BARLE

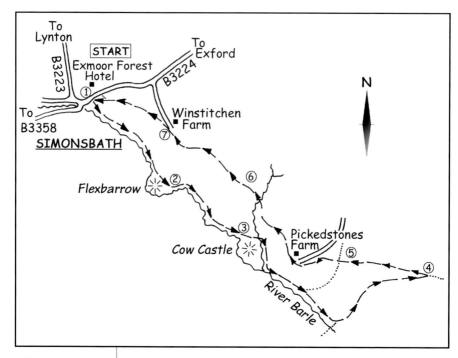

Distance:
7½ miles

Starting Point:
The free car park
to the rear of the
Exmoor Forest
Hotel in the centre
of Simonsbath.
GR 774392

Map: OS Explorer OL9 Exmoor

How to get there: *Simonsbath is 8 miles south of Lynton
on the B3223.*

*T*his is a delightful walk. It takes you from Simonsbath, where there is a choice of the Exmoor Forest Hotel and the Crown Hotel for refreshment, up onto the high moor through magnificent woodlands and along a delightful stretch of the River Barle. There is a good chance of seeing the rare dipper, a black bird with a white bib that feeds by swimming along the streambed. Blue waymarkers conveniently mark both the outward and homeward journeys, making navigation easy. The homeward trip is along the hilltop of the valley giving wonderful views and opportunities to sight buzzards and one of the three herds of pure-bred Exmoor ponies which exist on this part of the moor.

The way Exmoor looks today, wild and open, with its stone walls and limited roads, can be credited to John Knight, an industrialist from the Midlands, who bought Exmoor Forest in 1818 and then set about making it accessible and manageable for farming. Until that time the small hamlet of Simonsbath had just one house, where the forest warden lived.

Knight's vision was to convert the forest to agricultural land and hence to feed the nation. He needed shepherds and ploughmen and these were accommodated in bothies at Simonsbath. He built 22 miles of metalled roads connecting Simonsbath to the world outside, built a 29-mile wall around his estate, and then drained and burned large areas. The face of Exmoor began to change with roads, houses and other aspects of the new infrastructure arising.

Over a 50-year period in the mid 19th century, Simonsbath grew to become a village with a church, a school and an inn. Nowadays it can boast two hotels and tea rooms. However, nature was the long-term winner. Knight's vision of rich agricultural land was never realised, due to the poor quality of the soil and the harsh winter conditions, but his efforts left us with Exmoor as we see it today.

Nearby, for those seeking a less adventurous walk, is a short woodland route featuring carvings of all kinds of birds and animals, the handiwork of a local park ranger. It's a great way to keep children amused as they track them down, and the walk described conveniently passes through this woodland on the return journey.

THE START OF THE WALK

**The Exmoor Forest Hotel** dates back to the 18th century as an inn and even earlier as a house. The interior is full of hunting memorabilia, being in the heart of Exmoor, its walls bedecked with magnificent antlers, paintings and pictures of local characters. There is a full menu on offer, including meat, fish, poultry, pasta, curries, ploughman's, soups and sweets. The food is very good and the range of the local Exmoor Ales proves popular. Well-behaved dogs are allowed inside, and there is ample outdoor table space. Accommodation is available.

Telephone: *01643 831341.*

The Walk

① Leaving the car park, cross the road and head downhill towards the bridge over the **River Barle**. Pass through a gate on your left signposted to '**Wheal Eliza, Cow Castle, Landacre** and **Withypool**'. In a few yards, going uphill, take the right-hand path signposted along a blue waymarked route to '**Landacre via Cow Castle**' and follow this path as it runs parallel alongside the River Barle. This takes you along the lower side of **Birchcleeve Wood**, which despite its name is mostly beech.

② The path, the **Two Moors Way**, follows the **Barle** until, at the hill **Flexbarrow**, it leaves the river and then rejoins it near the site of the shaft of the disused **Wheal Eliza Mine**, at a point where a footbridge (which you ignore) crosses the river.

You are now entering the area of the tragic story of Anna Burgess who lived nearby with her father, in a cottage alongside the White Water, which you cross just a little further on. William Burgess, a sheep stealer and con man, murdered his daughter and buried her on the moor. Fearing her body would be discovered, he then threw it down the 75 metre deep mine shaft at the Wheal Eliza mine, where there had previously been an unsuccessful attempt to set up a copper mining business. The local vicar soon realised that the missing Anna had probably been murdered. Clues led to the mine shaft, which was pumped dry and her body discovered. William Burgess was later arrested in Wales and hanged in 1858 at Taunton for murder.

③ Continue along the same path as it follows the river and the blue waymarkers. Once more, it makes a detour away from the river as it passes around **Cow Castle**.

Cow Castle stands proud above the river and was once an Iron Age fort. On its summit, the remains of the walls are still visible, as much as 9 ft high, and provide an excellent viewpoint. Alongside Cow Castle is a smaller mound known as The Calf.

The path eventually moves back to track the river again, passing along the right-hand side of a plantation, following the blue markers through the woodland, before it starts to climb through bracken and heather as it bears away from the river towards a ridge. Turn left after passing through a field gate and proceed to the ridge.

④ At the ridge, take some time to admire the view, especially eastwards towards **Landacre Bridge**, then turn sharp left, signposted '**Simonsbath via Pickedstones**', and follow the blue waymarkers along the top of the valley until you reach a gate.

⑤ Pass through the gate and bear left (ignoring the metal gate almost immediately on your left) along the left-hand edge of the field. Pass through another gate on the far side of the field and then turn left along the farm track (following the

COW CASTLE

blue waymarked signpost to 'Pickedstones and Simonsbath') through another metal gate, and down towards the farm. Immediately before the farm, pass through the wooden gate following the blue waymarked sign to Simonsbath. Follow the short track through another field gate.

Bear right and follow the hedge on your right-hand side, passing through yet more gates and going downhill until you cross the White Water stream. Follow the track up the other side of the valley.

⑥ As you approach the top of the ridge, go left (signposted to Simonsbath with a blue mark) to pass to the left of two gate posts (again signposted with blue) and then bear right to follow the right-hand side of the field along which runs a small copse. Pass through three more gates. After the third gate, turn right to follow the right-hand field boundary.

The Exmoor pony, which you may see hereabouts, is one of the world's oldest breeds. These hardy animals have learnt to survive the harsh winters of the high moorland, when they can be seen with snow on their backs and frost on their manes. Usually brown or bay in colour, they are distinctive from other ponies by the mealy nose which looks as though it has just dipped into a bag of oatmeal. Unchanged for thousands of years, these are the ponies that King Arthur and his predecessor would have ridden and still make excellent riding ponies, standing at just over 12 hands.

⑦ Just before the next gate, bear left and then continue along the right-hand field boundary until, after bearing right, you pass through a gate into the next field. Continue with the hedge and wire field boundary on your right, passing through three more gates.

Bear left after the third gate and follow the left-hand field boundary to another gate. Pass through that gate and the next one just a few yards on, still waymarked with blue.

PICKSTONES FARM, HIGH ON EXMOOR

EXMOOR PONIES WITH THEIR OATMEAL-COLOURED NOSES

Follow the edge of the field on your right downhill until you pass through another gate to re-enter **Birchcleave Wood**.

Bear left to follow a path through the wood, signposted to

Simonsbath. Then bear right and follow the signposted path to the village and back to the road, across which you will see the **Exmoor Forest Hotel**.

Date walk completed:

WITHYPOOL AND TARR STEPS

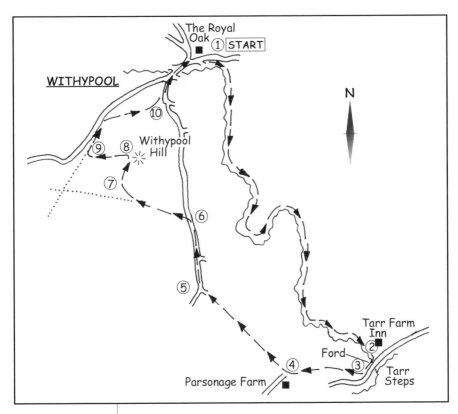

Distance:
9½ miles

Starting Point:
The Royal Oak car
park, Withypool.
GR 847356

Map: OS Explorer OL9 Exmoor

How to get there: *Withypool can be found just off the B3223, 6 miles north of Dulverton. The Royal Oak is in the centre of the village at the junction of the roads to Exford and Winsford. Cars may be left in the car park whilst you go on your walk but please let the owners know your expected time of return. Otherwise roadside park where practical.*

*T*his picturesque walk takes the Two Moors Way south from Withypool, following the fast flowing River Barle down to Tarr Steps and its famous clapper bridge. Withypool is tucked away in a wooded valley on the River Barle and until the 17th century it was the capital of Exmoor. Today, thanks to the difficulty of access for coaches, it remains largely unspoilt. Winters here can be cruel. In 1947, it was ten weeks before anyone could leave the village. Two prehistoric sites – a stone circle of 37 stones, erected in the Bronze Age, and a burial mound – are passed on the return journey on Withypool Hill. Withypool can now boast just the one shop and one inn. Across the road from the shop is a tea garden, open from Easter to October. There are also some rarely-seen 'Shell' petrol pumps, standing as if just waiting for a film company to spot their potential talents in a period drama. A picnic spot will be found alongside the six-arch stone bridge which crosses the River Barle, and there is a lovely riverside walk north from here towards Landacre and Simonsbath. South-west of the village, the skyline is dominated by Withypool Common and Withypool Hill, which stands at over 1,300 feet and over which this walk passes.

Whilst the featured pub is in Withypool, the Tarr Farm Inn provides a convenient halfway watering hole, with inn and tea gardens combined. Just a matter of yards off the route is also the excellent, remote Parsonage Farm, where homely cream teas are served.

The Royal Oak inn has been a focal point in the centre of Withypool for over 300 years and is ideally suited to the needs of the walker. It was once owned by Maxwell Knight, the spymaster who inspired the James Bond stories. In the 1800s R. D. Blackmore is believed to have written much of his novel *Lorna Doone* whilst staying here. His reservation is displayed on the wall. Another famous visitor was General Eisenhower, who stayed here in 1944 whilst visiting American troops in the area. The food is excellent, with a wide choice on the menu. Exmoor Ale and Exmoor Gold are the regular ales. The lounge bar is especially cosy in the winter months with its large wood fire. Accommodation is available and well-behaved dogs are welcome.

Telephone: *01643 831506.*

THE ROYAL OAK AT WITHYPOOL

 *The Walk*

① From the **Royal Oak**, head uphill until you reach a signpost indicating the **Two Moors Way** off to the right, following a yellow waymarked route to **Tarr Steps**. Climb the stile to take this path. Continue downhill to cross another stile and follow the path through the small wood. Cross two more stiles and a stream. From here on you follow the riverbank for 3½

miles all the way to the unmistakable **Tarr Steps**.

Tarr Steps is a 55-metre-long set of seventeen enormous flat stones which form a clapper bridge crossing the River Barle. As the nation's finest example of a clapper bridge, it is naturally an ancient monument. The largest stone is almost nine feet long and five feet wide and no form of bonding is used – it is simply the great weight of the stones which keeps them positioned as they should be. This was sufficient to hold them in place for hundreds of years until the winter of 1943, when the river froze and dislodged the stones. Then in 1952, the night that Lynmouth suffered its disastrous flood, storm water 12-feet deep swept away many of the stones. They were later replaced by the Royal Engineers.

Their origin is unknown but it is reasonable to consider that they date back to the Ice Age, a theory which ties in nicely with the nearby presence of Bronze Age burial mounds. In medieval times, they were used by pack-horse traders, and the stones were known as the Devil's Bridge, local legend having it that the bridge was built by the devil himself. He apparently still owns the bathing rights and, when a local vicar sent a black cat across the bridge in order to test whether or not it was safe to cross, the cat disappeared in a puff of smoke! Fortunately for walkers, the vicar, aware of the danger, crossed the bridge himself and returned the torrent of abuse from the devil with his own, even stronger, language. The devil conceded defeat and left the bridge.

COTTAGES AT WITHYPOOL

② Cross the clapper bridge. Avoid the footpath to the right which follows the river. Instead immediately after, where the road forks, go right and sharply uphill, signposted to **Withypool** and **Hawkridge**. In 80 yards, fork right (waymarked in blue) to avoid the hotel and follow the steep stony track uphill, ignoring the gates to left and right.

③ Pass through a gate and follow the sunken track, which bears to the right. Follow this track to a gate but, just before the gate, bear left, as indicated by a blue arrow, keeping the field boundary on your right-hand side. Continue until a field gate appears before you. Pass through this and keep in the same direction, but now with the field boundary on your left. Pass through another gate and field in the same fashion, again following the blue arrow.

④ At the next gate, at the entrance to **Parsonage Farm**, turn right, signposted **Withypool Hill**.

Parsonage Farm is well worth a short diversion of a few yards off the route. This remote Exmoor farm provides wonderful views down through a valley, which can be enjoyed as you tuck into home-grown, home-cooked food. Making a living is tough for such remote farms. In severe winters, this farm can become completely isolated,

and, in drought years, the spring-water drawn from its own well is limited, and water for the cattle has to be collected in tractor buckets from the stream further down the valley. It is no wonder that the couple who run the farm offer such a warm Exmoor welcome.

Keeping to the left-hand field boundary, pass through two more gates. After the second, bear slightly right and keep to the right-hand field boundary to reach a stile alongside a gate. Cross through and follow the signpost to '**Withypool** via **Withypool Hill**', going between a wire fence to the left and trees to your right. Continue downhill and pass through a metal gate. Head straight across the middle of the next field. Pass through the next metal gate, which brings you on to a lane.

⑤ Turn right onto the lane to pass **Westwater Farm** on your right.

⑥ In ½ mile, just after the cattle grid, turn left to follow a track that runs parallel with the hedge bank on your left. In about another ½ mile, the hedge bank finishes. Here you need to bear right and, with no path to follow, head uphill across the open moor. Watch out for a circle of stones.

This is a Bronze Age circle, 36 metres across. It was officially counted as 37 stones when discovered in 1898, although I counted 40! Whilst the stones are normally easy to spot, especially after the bracken has been burned, they can disappear from view when the bracken and heather are high, standing at the

A DRY STONE WALL ALONG THE BARLE VALLEY

most just a couple of feet high. If they are difficult to spot, then the best way is to find them from the top of Withypool Hill by taking a direct line to Tudball Splats across the valley on the opposite slope.

⑦ At the stones, bear slightly right to head uphill to the tumulus at the top of **Withypool Hill**.

⑧ At the **tumulus**, turn left to head west, following a path downhill until you reach a wide track.

⑨ Turn right on the track until it reaches a road. At this point, bear

right, slightly away from the road, onto a track that follows the contour line around **Withypool Hill**. Various paths criss-cross along the next stretch but just keep more or less in line with the road. Eventually drop downhill by bearing slightly left towards a large house.

⑩ Turn left onto the lane, which you should join by a small parking area. Follow the lane downhill into the village of **Withypool**, turning right on reaching the B road. Pass the cattle grid, **post office** and **church** to reach the **Royal Oak**.

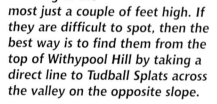

Date walk completed:

WINSFORD AND THE DEVIL'S PUNCHBOWL

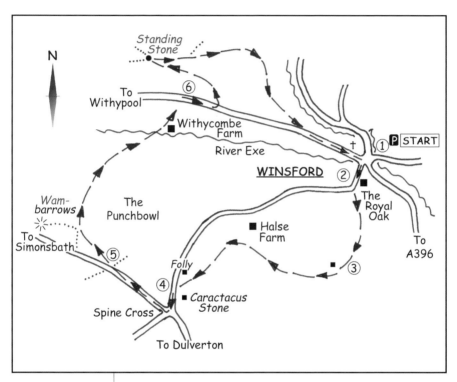

Distance:
7 miles

Map: OS Explorer OL9 Exmoor

Starting Point:
The free car park
by the village
green in the centre
of the village.
GR 906349

How to get there: *On the A396 between Dunster and Tiverton, a few miles south of Wheddon Cross, take the minor road west signposted to Winsford.*

THE ROYAL OAK INN, WINSFORD

The **Royal Oak Inn**, possibly the most picturesque pub in Somerset, began life in the 12th century as a farmhouse and dairy. Through the medieval period it served as a resting place for the packhorse travellers carrying their loads of wool along the trails across the moors. In time it took on its present role. This quintessential thatched village inn sits alongside the village green and Winn Brook. During the 17th century, the famous highwayman Tom Faggus was reputed to have held up travellers nearby, and the inn features in R. D. Blackmore's novel *Lorna Doone*. A warmer welcome is promised these days.

With three lounges and two bars, meals can be taken in the formal setting of the restaurant or light meals and Sunday lunches can be taken in the bars. Real ales include Brakspear and Butcombe's in this true walkers' pub where walking boots are likely to line the porchway as you enter. Well-behaved dogs are allowed in the bar. Accommodation is available in 14 bedrooms.

Telephone: *01643 851455.*

*T*his walk is particularly scenic and has the added attraction of passing a number of points of significant archaeological interest, including the Caractacus Stone in its shelter at Spire Cross and the Wambarrows, three ancient burial mounds on Winsford Hill. Watch out for buzzards, jays, red deer and Exmoor ponies as you stride out on the open moorland, past streams and deep-cut combes, and enjoy the wonderful views. Winsford is a charming village on the edge of the Exmoor National Park and dates back to the time of the Domesday Book. It boasts one shop, a tearoom and an inn. The village has changed very little in recent times and is one of those unspoilt corners of Exmoor. It sits on the River Exe and the Winn Brook with their eight bridges, including a packhorse bridge, and everything focuses around the village green. Ernest Bevin, trade union leader, wartime Minister of Labour, and Foreign Secretary, was born here in 1881. His birthplace across from the post office is marked with a plaque. One of the oldest buildings in the village is the Karslake House Hotel, which was a malthouse in the 15th century. One of its rooms still retains the original stone malt-drying floor. What used to be the school-house now contains the Community Computing Centre, providing public access to the Internet.

 *The Walk*

① From the car park, take the road that runs uphill past the **war memorial** and the thatched **Royal Oak Inn**.

② In a short distance, just after **Pippins** and **Hartland**, turn left onto a footpath signposted to **Dulverton**, **Tarr Steps** and **Winsford Hill**. The track soon bears right and ascends through high-banked hedgerows before dropping gently to a gate just before a brook.

③ Go through the gate and, ignoring the stile on the left, walk straight ahead, keeping just to the left of the boundary of **Yellowcombe Cottage**. A faint but identifiable path traces the cottage boundary to the right. Follow this round with the cottage on your right and brook on your left until the path crosses the brook. Then follow the path upstream, keeping the brook on your right-hand side.

In ¼ mile, watch out for a point where the stream splits. Here you can see a distinct track going off to the left. Take this path so that you follow the right-hand fork of the stream but keeping to its left-hand side. A fence separates you from the stream and pastureland on the other side. You will soon see **Halse Farm** to your right. Continue along the path, following the stream, until, in ¼ mile, bearing slightly left to take higher ground above the stream, signposted to **Folly**. In about ½ mile, you emerge from the trees onto open bracken-covered moorland. Continue along the uphill path to a metal gate. Go through this and straight ahead along a stony track to reach a metalled road in just a few yards.

Just a short distance to the left of here, before the crossroads, is the Caractacus Stone, which is protected by a stone shelter. Dating back to the 5th or 6th century, it stands 3 ft high and carries the Celtic inscription 'Descendant of Caractacus'. Caractacus was a British chieftain who led a rebellion against the Romans in AD 47–51. He was captured and taken to Rome, where he was paraded through the streets in chains. It is believed the stone was erected around AD 54, not so much to celebrate King Caractacus's one-time victory over the Romans, but to boost the local standing of one of his kinsmen.

Evidence shows that in 1219, the stone was used as a forest boundary and was called the 'Langeston', or Long Stone. It marked part of a route out of the Exe valley. In 1906, a shelter was built to protect it from the harsh winter weather, but it didn't stop vandals painting it in 2004 as a protest against the National Trust. Legend tells how a local carter once tried to dig for treasure believed to be hidden beneath the stone, but the stone toppled and crushed him. His ghost and that of a coach and horses are reputed to haunt this spot.

④ Turn left to reach the **Spine Cross** road junction, where you turn right, direction **Simonsbath** and **Lynton**, **Exford** and **Withypool**. Follow this metalled road as it climbs gently to a point where a well-defined path cuts across the road.

⑤ Turn right here, signposted **Withycombe**. In about 200 yards, at a crossroad of paths, turn right to head along the left-hand side of the deeply cut combe known as the **Punchbowl** and follow this path as it descends towards **Winn Brook**.

At this point, just before turning right, you can if you wish walk straight ahead to the crest of the hill, where a stone marks the site of three Bronze Age burial mounds, the Wambarrows. These

THE VILLAGE GREEN AT WINSFORD

three large barrows lie east to west. The most westerly is the largest, about 30 metres across.

You can then retrace your path to pick up the route as before. At the bottom of the combe can be seen Withycombe Farm. This is your target and the road leading up the hill behind the farm is also part of the route yet to come.

On reaching the boundary between open moorland and pasture, pass through the gate (waymarked in blue) and follow the right-hand field boundary. In the bottom corner of the field, pass through a blue waymarked gate and turn left to follow the left-hand field boundary to another blue-marked gate. Pass through this, turn right onto the farm track and follow it up to **Ash Lane**.

Take a look back at this point to view the Punchbowl.

(6) Turn right onto the road. In about 300 yards, just before the road bears left, there are two adjacent gates on the left-hand side. Take the first of

33

these, waymarked blue and signposted as the bridleway to **Nethercote** via **Bye Common**. Follow the right-hand field boundary to the next gate. Go through, turn left and follow the left-hand field boundary through the first field and into the second.

As you enter the second field, the boundary to your right runs downhill to a gate in the next corner and you are heading towards that gate. However, the official footpath takes you straight ahead to a **standing stone** and adjacent signpost. Proceed to the signpost and then almost double-back to the right, following the pointer for '**Winsford** via **Larcombe Foot**'.

In the bottom left-hand corner of the field, pass through the gate and continue straight ahead, keeping close to the field boundary on your right. Bear right off the main track, following the signpost to **Winsford**, and follow the same boundary to another gate. Continue beyond the gate to the end of the path.

Turn right through one gate and immediately left through another. Keep straight ahead with woodland on your left. At the corner of the field, turn left to follow the footpath sign down through the woods. Follow this path all the way down to the metalled road, ignoring the track to the left signposted to Exford. At the road, turn left to walk back into the centre of **Winsford** village.

Date walk completed:

DULVERTON AND THE RIVER BARLE

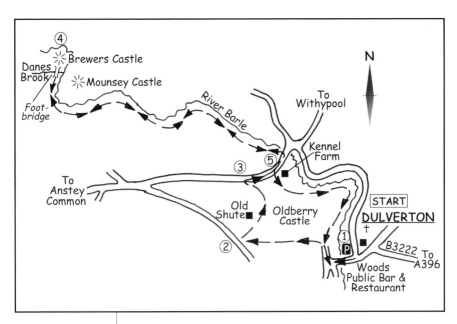

Distance:
9 miles

Map: OS Explorer OL9 Exmoor

Starting Point:
The 'pay and display' car park by the bridge crossing the River Barle in the centre of Dulverton. GR 912279

How to get there: *From the A396 between Tiverton and Minehead/Dunster, turn west onto the B3222, which leads into Dulverton village. Follow the road downhill to reach the river and turn right before the bridge into the free car park.*

WOODS PUBLIC BAR AND RESTAURANT, DULVERTON

Woods Public Bar and Restaurant, a wonderful country pub, will be found in Bank Square. From the river, walk up through the High Street and head towards the church. The pub is on your right, next to the Lion Hotel. Paddy Groves, former master of the Quantock Staghounds, has converted this old bakery to a truly rural bar, only recently opened. Outside you will find pick-up trucks and Land Rovers and inside the locals, with gun-dogs at heel. The walls have been stripped back to their timber framework and on the stone and timber floor stand wooden bench seats alongside heavy wooden tables. There is a wide choice of local real ales and the food is so fresh the menu is only published minutes before it becomes available. Ask about the meat dishes on offer and you will most likely be given the full details... 'It's a Devon Red sirloin. Real organic. Ask him. He's the butcher', as your host points towards one of his customers. Woods Public Bar is a wonderful addition to Dulverton, where walking boots and well-behaved dogs will be given a warm welcome.

Telephone: *01398 324007.*

*M*uch of this very pleasant walk, which starts and finishes at the riverside car park, hugs the bank of the tree-lined River Barle. The detour from the river at the start of the walk takes you around the bounds of Oldberry Castle fort and later you climb to the top of another Iron Age fort to enjoy outstanding views. Watch out for dippers along the riverside walk. Dulverton is at the heart of Exmoor and its connections with the story of Lorna Doone are reflected by her statue at the entrance to the car park. The town stands between the two rivers of the Barle and the Exe, which converge about a mile downstream from the town. This places Dulverton right in the heart of excellent walking country and it is also perhaps the best place for the visitor to do any essential shopping, since it has a post office, butcher's shop, bank, fish and chip shop, greengrocer's, late-night supermarket, and a gun and fishing tackle shop, which you would expect in the heart of hunting territory. Alongside the river Barle are the headquarters of the Exmoor National Park Authority, a useful information centre for walkers. The five-arched bridge that spans the river is an ancient monument and a favourite place for children to play during the summer months. The 13th century church is well worth a visit and almost next door to the Woods Public Bar!

DULVERTON'S BRIDGE OVER THE RIVER BARLE

THE TOWN HALL AT DULVERTON

 *The Walk*

① From the car park, return to the five-arched river **bridge** and turn right to cross the **River Barle**. Turn immediately right again and follow the waymarked route signposted to **Beech Tree Cross**. The waymarks lead you across fields and onto a farm drive, which brings you out at **Beech Tree Cross**.

② On reaching the road, turn right

to follow the track waymarked to **Old Shute**, but ignore the track eventually going left to **Old Shute**, and continue to the right, keeping the heights of **Oldberry Castle** on your right, to reach the metalled road.

③ Turn right and follow the road, past **Kennel Farm** on your right, to **Marsh Bridge** and the **River Barle**. Just before the bridge, turn left, signposted to **Hawkridge** and **Tarr Steps**. Follow the riverside path through wonderful woodland,

LORNA DOONE'S STATUE AT THE RIVERSIDE CAR PARK

keeping the river on your right-hand side.

④ In 2 miles, you reach **Castle Bridge**, which crosses **Danes Brook** as it runs down from **Anstey Common** on your left to join the **River Barle**. Cross the footbridge and follow the footpath marked to **Tarr Steps** just long enough to allow you to climb to the top of **Brewers Castle**, the high ground before you. Having taken in the views, retrace your steps back along the river to the metalled road at **Marsh Bridge**.

Brewers Castle and, across the river, Mountsey Castle are Iron Age hill forts. It is easy to see why they should have been placed where they are, with such commanding views.

⑤ On reaching the road, turn right to head back to **Kennel Farm**. At the farm, turn left into the farmyard and go through two gates to follow the waymarked riverside path all the way back to **Dulverton** and the car park.

Date walk completed:

TRISCOMBE AND THE QUANTOCK HILLS

THE BLUE BALL INN AT TRISCOMBE

Distance: 7 miles	**Map:** OS Explorer 22 Quantock Hills and Exmoor
Starting Point: The free car park opposite the Blue Ball Inn at Triscombe. GR 155355	**How to get there:** *Triscombe is just north of the A358 between Taunton and Williton and is signposted off this road. An alternative starting point is the car park at Triscombe Stone, halfway around the walk, found at the head of Cockercombe and most easily accessed from the road between Nether Stowey and Aisholt.*

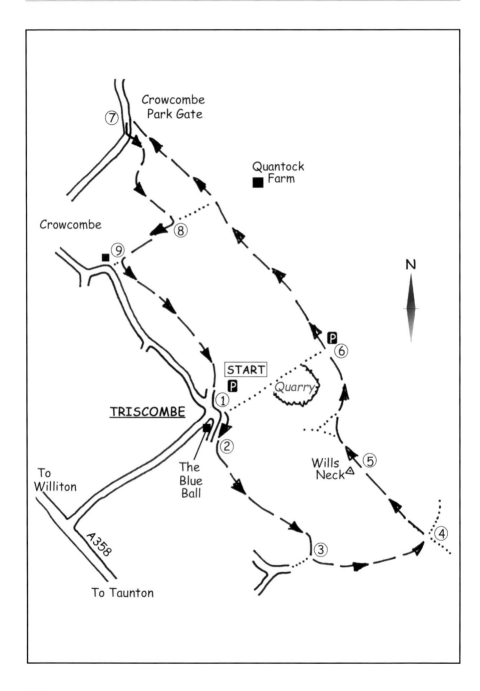

*T*his walk takes in the ridge and southwestern face of the Quantock Hills, passing through open moorland and visiting Wills Neck, the highest point on the Quantocks at 1,264 ft. Watch out for buzzards, red deer, signs of badgers (in the woodland on the latter part of the walk), and stonechats, which perch atop the gorse bushes, making a sound similar to that of two pebbles being clicked together. The Quantock Hills were the nation's first Area of Outstanding Natural Beauty. Deeply cleft combes with rich deciduous woodland combine with forestry plantations and open moorland to create a magnificent environment for the keen walker. This is hunting country and home to the Quantock Staghounds. The recent changes in legislation now permit the hunt to run only one pair of hounds at a time rather than the full pack. Nonetheless, they are a regular sight on these hills.

This is also the landscape which inspired Coleridge and the Wordsworths when they lived on these hills, a period during which they created their most inspired works. Coleridge lived in Nether Stowey, where his cottage, now in the hands of the National Trust, can be visited, whilst William and Dorothy Wordsworth lived at Alfoxden Park in nearby Holford. This is now a country hotel.

On this route there is one steep climb, which comes early in the walk as you ascend to the Quantock Ridge on the way to Wills Neck.

The **Blue Ball Inn** at Triscombe is a wonderful thatched country inn that welcomes walkers. To cater for wet weather, as you enter, there is a shelf on which muddy boots can be placed and no one will mind your walking socks. Well-behaved dogs are also welcome. In fine weather, you can enjoy the attractive landscaped, lawned garden. The food, traditional fayre coming from a fine à la carte menu, is excellently prepared and presented, with seasonal vegetables.

The inn is a free house and provides local real ales. Cotleigh Tawny is the resident, with Exmoor Ales, Otter Ales and Butcombe's appearing among the regular guest ales. This is hunting territory and the interior of the inn is bedecked with pictures of foxes, otters, hounds and stag antlers. Two letting rooms are available

Telephone: *01984 618242.*

The Walk

① On leaving the car park, turn left and then immediately right to take the road which runs up behind the **Blue Ball Inn**, signposted to **West Bagborough**. The road bears left and goes uphill.

② At the point where the road bears right and appears to go downhill, take the track to the left and continue gradually uphill. Ignore the gated track that bears off left and continue along the signposted footpath, dropping gradually downhill until you cross a stream where a small white cottage can be seen to the left. Continue along the path until, dropping downhill, you see a gate that leads into a lane and to **Rock Farm**.

③ A few yards before reaching the gate, turn sharp left to head steeply back uphill. Ignore the gated lane

A THATCHED BARN AT TRISCOMBE

that crosses your path and continue uphill.

④ In about ½ mile you reach the crest of the hill, just after emerging from the woods. Here you will find a small pond on the right-hand side by the tree line.

The pond is an evening watering hole for the wild ponies that wander the hills. Although each pony is owned by one of the local farmers, they roam as wild animals. In September each year, the spring-born foals and their mares are rounded up and then the foals are auctioned in one of the nearby villages. Pony lovers always hope that the foals reach good prices, since a low price suggests they may end up as pet food rather than pet. They make excellent riding ponies, especially for children.

Just a few yards after this, a wide path crosses yours as it runs along the **Quantock ridge**. Turn left onto this ridge path. In about 100 yards, the track splits. Take the right-hand path. Continue along this track until you reach the triangulation point at **Wills Neck**.

Wills Neck is the highest point on the Quantock Hills at over 1,260 ft above sea level and offers wide views across Exmoor on one side

and to the coast of South Wales on the other.

⑤ After the triangulation point, the path splits. Take the right-hand path, which leads downhill, gradually approaching the woods to your right.

⑥ On reaching the tree line bear left, keeping to the bold path that drops downhill, and skirts the quarry to your left. Continue along the track to where it joins another, more obvious, track just after a wooden bench seat. Turn left here onto the main track and ignore the roads to left and right at the cattle grid.

Here you will find the car park at Triscombe Stone, which is the alternative start for your walk. If you have parked here, then your directions are to cross the cattle grid from the car park, turn right onto the tree-lined track and continue as below.

Triscombe Stone is an ancient stone with all kinds of associated legends, mostly to do with the Devil. Please note, it's the stone that stands alongside your track and not the man-made stone in the centre of the car park area.

Continue straight ahead along the tree-lined path, which follows the Quantock ridge for 1½ miles, until you reach the metalled road at **Crowcombe Park Gate**.

TILTING BEECH TREES ALONG THE QUANTOCK RIDGE

Notice the isolated Quantock farms to your right as you pass along this ridge path. Snow settles more readily on this higher ground and these farms can be quite inaccessible during severe winters. At Crowcombe Park Gate, on most summer weekends, there is an ice cream van! To find it, turn right at the metalled road. In a few yards you reach a stony parking area to your left.

⑦ You now begin your return journey. Turn left at the road to cross the cattle grid and pass through the metal gate immediately on your left. In about 100 yards, bear right onto the track across the field, to go up and over the ridge before you. As the path swings left, you cross the ridge to drop down into **Little Quantock Combe**.

QUANTOCK HILLS MARE AND FOAL

⑧ On reaching the trough of the combe, pass through a field gate and then turn right to follow the stony track downhill.

Turn left before the farm gate onto a path that takes you uphill. As you approach the ridge, the path splits. Take the right fork heading towards the wooded area. The path forks again. Take the right fork, heading towards where the hedge on your right meets the woodland before you.

Along this section of the walk you may well hear the whistle of a steam train. Looking to your right, down into the valley, you should see the steam from the engines travelling on the West Somerset Railway. This section of railway ran from Taunton to Minehead as early as 1874 but was axed by Dr Beeching in 1971. In 1975, however, the West Somerset Railway came to the rescue and, by 1979, steam trains were running from Bishops Lydeard to Minehead. Twenty scenic miles in length, it is the longest privately owned passenger line in the country. It now employs around 30 people plus a number of volunteers. In 1964, Beatlemania hit Minehead when the Beatles recorded part of their first movie, A Hard Day's Night, using the steam trains and Crowcombe and Minehead stations. More recently, the station at Minehead hosted the Antiques Roadshow.

Just to the left of where the hedge meets the wood, pass through a gate into the trees. The obvious path eventually leads you down into **Triscombe Combe**. On reaching the bottom of the combe, turn right and almost immediately pass through a gate to emerge onto a road. Turn left here and in a matter of yards you arrive at your car park and the **Blue Ball Inn**.

 Date walk completed:

COMBWICH AND BRIDGWATER BAY

THE ANCHOR INN, COMBWICH

Distance: 8½ miles	Map: OS Explorer 22 Quantock Hills and Exmoor
Starting Point: Gravel lay-by beside the river, close to the Anchor Inn, Combwich. GR 260424	**How to get there:** *From the A39 Bridgwater to Minehead road, take the road into Cannington village and then, in the village centre, turn uphill signposted Combwich and Hinkley Point. As the main road bears left, turn right, signposted Combwich. Just follow the road into the village. When the road bears sharp left, go straight on to the riverbank and the Anchor Inn.*

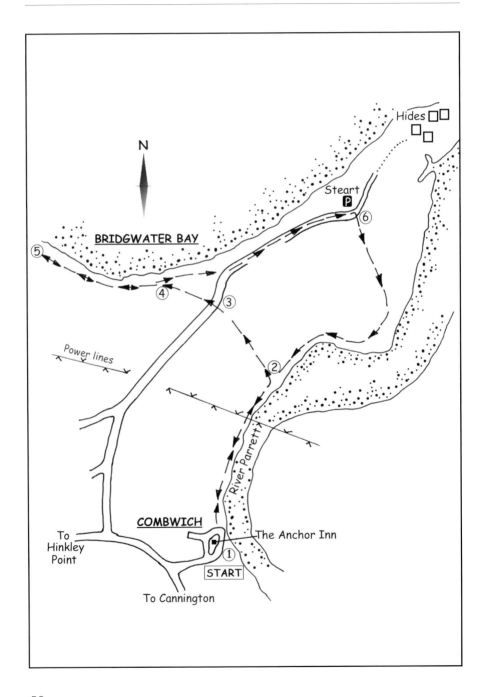

Hides

N

BRIDGWATER BAY

Steart
P
⑥

⑤

④

③

Power lines

②

River Parrett

COMBWICH

To
Hinkley
Point

The Anchor Inn

①

START

To Cannington

*T*his walk follows the lovely River Parrett down to its mouth in the Bristol Channel. Part of the route is just a few feet above sea level, through lush grasslands. The walk takes in Bridgwater Bay, a nature reserve of international importance. This is the wintering ground for thousands of shelduck. Also during the winter months a host of other wildfowl can be seen including large flocks of wigeon and teal plus shoveller and pochard. Over 190 species have been recorded from the observation hides, from which huge flocks of knot and dunlin can be watched as they swirl around over the shore-line as if all attached to one other. Over the years I have seen little egret, the occasional spoonbill, avocets, snow bunting and all kinds of rarities at the reserve. Foxes, badgers and hares can also be seen on a good day. The river is subjected to twice-daily tides with a rise and fall of some 30 ft. Because of the rapidly narrowing shape of the Rivers Severn and Parrett, they are swept by the bore, a tidal wave that runs up the river about 1 hour and 40 minutes after low water. During the high spring and autumn tides, it may be worth timing your walk so that the first 2 miles coincide with this phenomenon. Bird watchers may also prefer to start their walk about an hour before high tide, when the maximum amount of birdlife is close to the high-water shoreline.

The **Anchor Inn** at Combwich dates back to the late 18th century, albeit much altered in the 1950s to provide the appearance of a ship's deck along the frontage. The timbered-ceiling bars contain a selection of maritime memorabilia, reminding the visitor of the one-time significance of Combwich as a seaport.

A selection of real ales is available, such as Cotleigh's and Cousin Jack. Food is available at lunchtime from Wednesday to Sunday only. The lunchtime menu is also limited, to perhaps fish and chips, jacket potatoes and similar, but the evening menu is much more varied. Well-behaved dogs are permitted in the bar.

Telephone: *01278 653612.*

The Walk

① Facing the river, turn left to follow the riverside bridleway. For most of the way there is a choice of two parallel paths, one along the top of the riverbank that provides views of the river, and one at the base of the riverbank that becomes a gravel track. Follow the path along the top of the river wherever possible. After passing under a line of electricity pylons, in about ¼ mile, you reach the **North Clyce**.

② At this point, a gate crosses the river embankment path and is signposted for the **River Parrett Trail**. Ignore this, since this will be your return path. Down to your left is a metal gate at an entrance to a large rectangular field. Cross this and head half-left to the opposite corner of the field, in the direction of a telegraph pole, to cross into the next field.

Keep in the same general direction as the field narrows, until you reach a gate on the far side, which leads out onto a single-track road.

③ Cross the road, still heading in the same general direction. You will see a large area of common before you with a raised bank, the common wall, along the left-hand side. Follow this until it joins the track that runs parallel with the coast, just inside the **sea wall embankment**.

④ Turn left to follow the coast towards the clearly visible **Hinkley Point Nuclear Power Station**. Eventually you will pass a long lagoon on your left, followed by a stone wall. Follow the path to the end of the stone wall and then go up onto the raised bank to commence your return trip.

SMALL CRAFT MOORED IN THE CREEK AT COMBWICH

A NAVIGATION BUOY AT COMBWICH PILL

The lagoon offers several species of birds: various warblers, plus coot, moorhen and dabchick. This is a fresh water lagoon. Go quietly as you walk to the top of the embankment. On the other side are saltwater lagoons and it is quite common to see little egrets, herons and a host of wading birds. Curlew are very common, along with redshank, knot, dunlin and oyster catchers. Please remember that one noisy visitor can frighten these away and they take a long time to settle back.

Hinkley Point nuclear power station is rarely out of the local news. There are two power generating units: Hinkley A, the large single building nearest to you, which has now closed down; and the two giant towers of Hinkley B. The latter, at the time of writing, is partially closed down and will probably remain on reduced output due to cracks in the pipework. A third station, Hinkley C, and a wind-farm adjacent to the site, are both on the agenda for the future, both proposals having equally vociferous supporters and objectors.

⑤ Turn right on the raised path to head back to the **common**. When the raised path becomes too pebbly, drop back down to the regular track and continue straight ahead keeping the shoreline to your left. On reaching the metalled road, continue straight ahead along the road into the hamlet of **Steart**, passing the chapel, various chicken sheds and farms until, on your left-hand side, you arrive at the **National Nature Reserve Visitors' Car Park**.

The walk can be extended to take in the bird observation hides at Steart Point.

⑥ In 40 yards, immediately opposite **Dowells Farm**, turn right onto a permissive pathway, a stony track that you follow all the way to its end at the bank of the **River Parrett**. Cross the gate at the end of the track, walk up onto the river bank, turn right and follow the track all the way back to your car at **Combwich** and the **Anchor Inn**.

 Date walk completed:

EAST BOWER
AND SEDGEMOOR

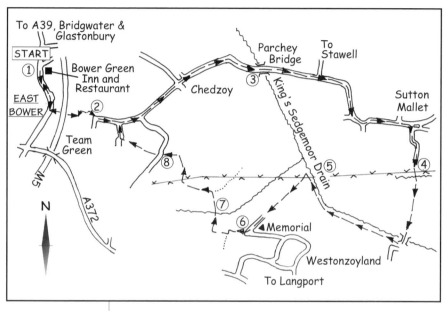

Distance:
9 miles

Starting Point:
*The Bower Green
Restaurant and
Inn, where you
can park with
the owner's
permission.
Alternatively the
small lay-by just
to the south of
the inn.
GR 321374*

Map: OS Explorer 22 Quantock Hills and Bridgwater

How to get there: *Bower Lane runs along the eastern
edge of Bridgwater, parallel with the M5 motorway. On
entering the town on the A39 from the east, Bower Lane is
on your left after the motorway bridge.*

THE BOWER GREEN INN AND RESTAURANT

*L*eaving the edge of Bridgwater, this fascinating walk crosses dairy and arable farmland, passing through the village of Chedzoy and on to Sutton Mallet. The return journey follows the line of King's Sedgemoor Drain. Watch out for roe deer, foxes, heron and lapwing. This is flat walking in the area where the last battle on English soil was fought, the Battle of Sedgemoor in 1685. Today it is dairy country, with fine Friesian herds. The land is drained with a network of rhynes, ditches and man-made rivers, or drains. At one time, the complete area of this walk would have flooded every winter, but this led to excellent summer grazing, hence the name of Somerset, the land of the summer people.

The Bower Green Restaurant and Inn is a relatively recent addition to the list of Somerset watering holes, having served as a farmhouse for most of its life. Although close to the motorway, which runs behind the inn, you will hardly be aware of the traffic. The garden makes this place rather special with its wishing well and flower-pot men climbing up the front wall. Well-behaved dogs and children are welcome. Real ales and an à la carte menu with daily specials are on offer. Accommodation is available.

Telephone: *01278 422926.*

The Walk

① From **Bower Green**, walk south along **Bower Lane** with the motorway on your left and a housing estate on your right. After passing a concrete barn on your left (lay-by parking), continue to a field gate with stile, signposted as the **Samaritans Way**. Turn left into the field, and head for the top left corner. Cross the small footbridge over the ditch and then cross the large footbridge over the motorway.

From here you can see three church towers – the one slightly to your left is Chedzoy, almost straight ahead is Sutton Mallet and slightly to your right is Westonzoyland. These mark the outer boundaries of the walk.

Once over the bridge, turn left at the bottom, as you exit the fenced area, to continue in your previous direction. Straight ahead of you, on the far side of the field, cross the **Summerway Rhyne** and turn left to reach a gate and dilapidated stile. Cross the gated entrance and then turn right and walk ahead, passing beneath the electricity pylons. On the other side of the field, as the hedge bears left, you will come to a small footbridge.

Turn right over this footbridge and head for the large ash tree directly opposite. (Should the field be planted with crops, it may be wise to follow the right-hand field boundary round to the bridge and then on to a stile and footbridge.)

② Pass through the stile and over the footbridge to enter the start of a drove. Ignore the bridleway that crosses your path and just keep straight ahead (**Portwall Drove**) and then onto a metalled road. Continue in the same direction into the village of **Chedzoy** (pronounced Chedzee).

The church of St Mary is well worth a visit. A 13th brass memorial to a knight will be found in the floor (usually by lifting an old mat which protects it), and another interesting feature is in fact one which is missing, or at

ALONG KING'S SEDGEMOOR DRAIN FROM PARCHEY BRIDGE

least has been since the summer of 2006. Just inside the church gates is a plinth which is supposed to support a half life-size bronze of a First World War soldier mounted on horse back. The statue of Sydney Mason Collins, who served with the Royal Signals in France and was mentioned in despatches, had adorned the churchyard since 1950, four years after the soldier's death. His family roots in Chedzoy can be traced back to the 16th century. The whereabouts of his statue is unlikely to be traced, having been stolen in an overnight raid and now almost certainly having been melted down.

This was one of the churches in which rebels were held prisoner after the Battle of Sedgemoor. By turning left just before the bend at the church, the Manor Inn can be found. A candle auction is held here every 21 years when the rights to Church Acre become available for rent.

Bear right at the church and continue until you reach **Parchey Bridge** to cross the **King's Sedgemoor Drain**.

The Drain was built in 1797 to draw off water from the surrounding moor for agricultural purposes, but it proved inadequate and hence, in 1861, a pumping station was added to the scheme. Nowadays this lengthy waterway is not only an excellent spot for angling, but also provides an important corridor for the movement of otters, which are slowly making a return to the area.

③ Continue ahead along the road, ignoring the left turn to Stawell and keeping straight on to **Sutton Mallet**. In a while the road twists and turns before entering the village, whose church tower you will have seen for some while. Turn right in the village to go past the church and go straight ahead into the 'No through road'.

Follow this road past **Nino's Farm**, **Dairy House Farm** and **Godfrey's Farm**. Just after Godfrey's Farm, bear right to follow a track, which drops steeply down to the levels as it heads south towards the **King's Sedgemoor Drain**.

④ At the bottom of the track, turn left and almost immediately right, passing under pylons as you do so. Continue straight ahead to cross a footbridge, and then straight ahead to cross the bridge over **King's Sedgemoor Drain**.

After crossing the bridge, turn immediately right to follow the left bank of **King's Sedgemoor Drain**. In about ¾ mile, the drain bends to the right and in about another ¼ mile you pass under the high power lines.

⑤ Shortly after this, turn left onto a track known as **Langmoor Drove**. Follow this to a T-junction.

On your right you will pass the memorial to those who fell at the Battle of Sedgemoor in 1685 and

ST MARY'S CHURCH AT CHEDZOY

at numerous other, some almost forgotten, battles. The Battle of Sedgemoor was the last battle fought on English soil and was the failed attempt of the Protestant James II, Duke of Monmouth, the illegitimate son of Charles II, to capture the throne of England from his Catholic uncle. The King's troops were well disciplined, battle hardened and outnumbered the rebel army of Monmouth, whose troops were mostly local volunteers, enthusiastic but untrained. Monmouth's only hope of success was by a night attack on the King's camp. His troops left Bridgwater just before midnight and made their way via Bawdrip and Chedzoy to the camp. There, at the critical moment, a musket was fired accidentally which alerted the King's troops, and Monmouth's troops suffered the consequences. Over a thousand men died on the battlefield, and most of them were buried in a mass grave. Thousands later suffered at the Bloody Assizes, and Monmouth himself was beheaded in the Tower of London.

⑥ Turn right and in about 300 yards, the track bears left. In a further 50 yards, turn right through a field gate and follow the left-hand field boundary to reach a gap in the corner of the field. Pass through the gap and turn immediately right to follow the right-hand field boundary until you reach the **New Chedzoy Cut Rhyne.**

⑦ Cross the cut using the footbridge, which is slightly to your left, and continue straight ahead, following the right-hand field boundary. On reaching the **Moor Drove** track, turn left and follow the track to the cluster of cottages at Fowler's Plot.

⑧ At the metalled road at **Fowler's Plot**, turn left and then right to go through the second gate, one field to the left of the cottages.
   Follow the right-hand field boundary until you come to a large wooden bridge with small stile. Head diagonally across the field to reach a farm track with hedgerows on each side. Turn right onto this drove and then in about 250 yards turn left at the T-junction of droves to retrace your step to **Bower Green**.

 Date walk completed:

STOKE ST GREGORY AND BURROW MUMP

THE ROSE AND CROWN AT WOODHILL, STOKE ST GREGORY

Distance:
7½ miles

Starting Point:
The Rose and
Crown at
Woodhill,
Stoke St Gregory.
GR 354273

Maps: OS Explorer 22 Quantock Hills and Bridgwater and
OS Explorer 128 Taunton and Blackdown Hills

How to get there: *From Burrowbridge on the A361
between Othery and Taunton, take the riverside road to
Stathe. In Stathe, turn right for Woodhill and Stoke St
Gregory. In 2 miles, turn left for Woodhill and the Rose and
Crown. Parking is limited at the pub but practical roadside
parking can be found nearby at the entrance to a drove, or
along the road.*

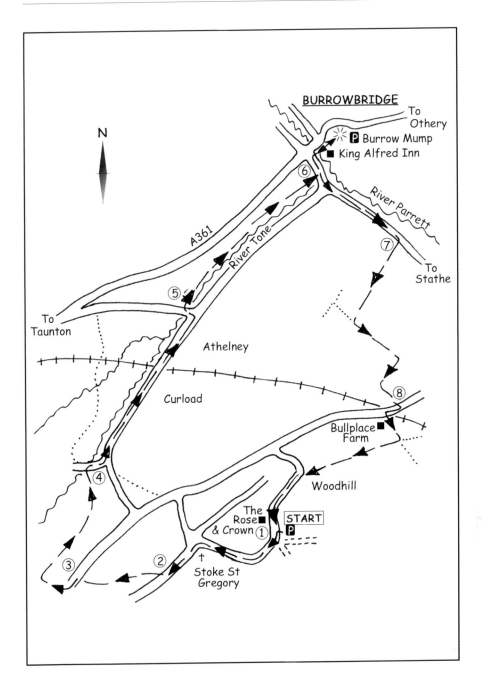

A flat and easy walk in the land of King Alfred that passes through the willow growing wetlands of Somerset. For part of the route, the River Parrett Trail is followed and is well waymarked. A choice of hostelries adorns the route with the Pigeons Inn at Curload and the King Alfred Inn at Burrowbridge adding to the chosen Rose and Crown. There are willow centres to visit at both Stoke St Gregory, where the Willow and Wetlands centre can be found, and Curload. The fields of willow will be self-evident along the route and these are used to produce a wide range of baskets, furniture and hurdles. Wicker products were very important throughout the war years. When supplies had to be parachuted into enemy territory, it was the locally-made wicker basket which provided the strength and resilience to withstand heavy landings without breaking open. They were often despatched containing letters from the young girls who made them, destined for the unknown soldiers who would receive them. This wicker has also been used for decades in the making of fishing creels and baskets, thanks again to their robustness and their ability to tolerate wet conditions.

Burrowbridge lies at the very heart of the Somerset Levels with Aller Moor, King's Sedgemoor, Curry Moor and West Sedgemoor surrounding Burrow Mump, a tor which, although small, dominates the landscape. During the winter, much of the area can lie deep under water for months at a time, and this makes it particularly attractive to wading birds such as lapwing, curlew and snipe. Because of its value to wildlife, much of the area is designated a Site of Special Scientific Interest.

The Walk

① Leaving the car park at the **Rose and Crown**, turn right towards **Stoke St Gregory**. The road bears round to the right and passes the church on the left. After the village shop, turn left round the corner and then left into **Huntham Lane**.

② In ¼ mile, turn right, opposite **Sturts Farm**, onto the signposted footpath.

You are now picking up the route of the River Parrett Trail, which should be signposted with 'eel' logos all the way back to Burrowbridge.

Stepping into the **Rose and Crown** at Woodhill, Stoke St Gregory, is like stepping into someone's home. It's not just the friendly welcome but the shape and structure. The inn is approached through a small garden with seven tables laid out on a patio area. Inside are small, homely rooms, with low beamed ceilings and the walls adorned with an assortment of memorabilia, including photos of local folk groups like the legendary Wurzels and Denver Spur. A good choice of food and real ales is on offer, with à la carte and daily specials, plus sandwiches and salads. An interesting internal feature is the glass-topped well in the middle of the bar. Accommodation is available. This village inn is deservedly very popular and booking is advised if you wish to use it for meals at weekends.

Telephone: *01823 490296.*

Cross the stile and follow the left-hand field boundary to the next stile with a footbridge. Cross this, follow the left-hand field boundary to a footbridge on your left. Go over this and turn half-right to reach the top right-hand corner to a stile and gate. Cross the stile, continue straight ahead through the next field and on to the metalled road.

③ Turn left onto the road and, in 200 yards, turn right over a cattle grid to follow a track and then walk straight ahead to a gate and stile. Cross the stile and follow the left-hand field boundary to a stile and steps. Cross the stile, turn right immediately to cross another stile. Follow the right-hand field boundary for two more fields. In about 600 yards, you will reach steps and a stile in the field corner. Cross the stile and go up the steps. On reaching a track,

turn left and go straight ahead between the sewage works and a hedge to reach a gate.
  Continue straight ahead through the gate, following the right-hand field boundary, through the next gate and straight ahead onto **Windmill Hill**, still following the right-hand field boundary to descend down to some farm buildings.

④ Turn left around the side of the building and then turn right to pass through a gate. Go straight ahead and then bear right to reach a stile in about 100 yards. Cross the stile and turn right onto the track that leads to the metalled road.

You could now take a diversion to visit the English Basket Centre.

Turn left onto the road, crossing the railway line and eventually turning left to cross the **River Tone**, signposted **Lyng**.

⑤ Immediately after crossing the river, turn right to follow the riverbank, with the river on your right, all the way to the road at Burrowbridge.

As you walk along the riverside, look to your left for an island of raised ground on which is placed the monument to King Alfred. It was here at Athelney that he burnt the cakes. In 870 AD, Danish Vikings, under their leader Guthrum, had overthrown the kingdoms of East Anglia,

Northumbria and Mercia. They were aiming to do the same to Alfred's Wessex. For several years, the struggling young Alfred was pushed back to the Somerset marshes, where he had his stronghold at Athelney. At his lowest ebb, Alfred was forced to travel incognito and sought shelter in a peasant woman's hut. Left with the simple chore of keeping an eye on cakes on a griddle, his thoughts wandered to how he was to overcome the Danes, and the cakes were neglected, earning him the wrath of the kindly peasant lady. But that was Alfred's turning point. Soon after, he defeated the

THE RUINED CHURCH OF ST MICHAEL ON BURROW MUMP

Danes and brought peace to his nation, introducing a system of fortified towns, or burghs, with each burgh never more than 20 miles from the next. He took London back from the Danes and re-established Saxon control of the south of England. His leadership was such that he was the only English king ever entitled 'the Great'.

⑥ At the road, turn left and then right to cross the **River Parrett**. Keep to the right-hand side of the road and shortly after the **King Alfred Inn** find a gateway on your right where a footpath leads you to **Burrow Mump**. You can climb to the top and take in one of the best all-round views in Somerset.

From here can be seen the Mendip Hills, the Blackdowns, the Quantocks and across the levels to the Bristol Channel.

Retrace your steps to point 6 but once there continue straight ahead, keeping the river on your left. Ignore the road to the right signposted to **Athelney** and **Curload**.

⑦ In about ½ mile, after passing a pumping station on your right and **Withy Orchard** on your left, turn right onto a track, **Brownings Drove**. In ½ mile, turn left at a T-junction onto **Bull Load Drove**. In about ¼ mile, this drove bends

sharp to the right, then left and right again, eventually reaching the metalled road.

⑧ Turn right onto the road, cross the railway line over the bridge and then turn immediately left just before **Bullplace Farm** onto another drove. In about 300 yards, the drove becomes unfenced on the left-hand side. At this point, take the second gate on your right. Follow the right-hand field boundary for two fields. In the second field, ignore the first gate on your right and continue ahead to the one in the corner of the field.

Pass through that gate and turn half-left to a gate in the opposite corner by a cattle trough. Go through the gate to enter a lane, turning right. Continue to where the lane bears right and keep straight ahead over a stile, and then a second stile. Continue straight ahead, pass through a gap in the corner of the field, and keep ahead, crossing the next stile to reach the road in **Woodhill**. Turn left to find the **Rose and Crown**.

Stoke St Gregory is the home of the Coates willow industry with its Willow and Wetlands Visitor Centre. It is well worth a visit.

Date walk completed:

HOLMAN CLAVEL AND THE BLACKDOWN HILLS

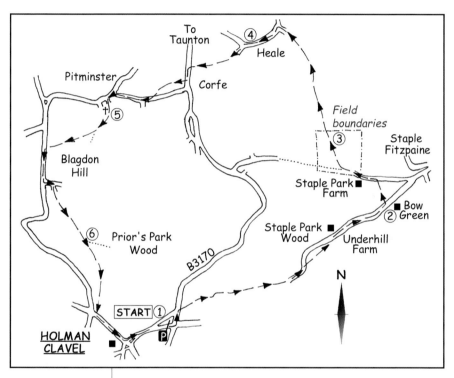

Distance:
10 miles

Map: OS Explorer 128 Taunton and Blackdown Hills

Starting Point:
Parking area to the east of the Holman Clavell inn on Blagdon Hill. GR 228163

How to get there: *From Taunton town centre, take the B3170 south, passing through the village of Corfe. After the right turn to Feltham, and after a left-hand bend, the road becomes unfenced on the left-hand side. Take the second turning right, signposted Churchingford. The first and second turnings come close to each other. The parking area will be on your right-hand side. About ⅓ mile further on is the Holman Clavel inn. Ample kerbside parking is available along this stretch of road.*

THE HOLMAN CLAVEL INN ON BLAGDON HILL

This walk explores the wild and ancient woodland areas of the Blackdown Hills, to the south of Corfe and Pitminster. The shape of the Blackdown Hills is a result of the geology of the district, with hard greensand rocks underlying the soil and creating a plateau from which valleys have been cut by the action of the water. The forests lining the valleys date back many hundreds of years and are some of the oldest woodlands in the country. Just a short distance from the county town of Taunton, the Blackdown Hills provide pleasant and adventurous walking. The villages are full of charm and offer a plentiful choice of inns. In addition to the isolated, and haunted, Holman Clavel, there is the White Hart at Corfe, the White Lion at Blagdon Hill, the Queen's Arms in Pitminster and, only slightly off the route, the Greyhound Inn at Staple Fitzpaine. Most inclines are gradual, the steepest coming towards the end and the Holman Clavel inn is the reward on that uphill stretch.

The **Holman Clavel** inn, with its beamed ceilings and wooden benches, dates back 600 years. The unusual name is from Old English 'holman' meaning made of holly, and 'clavel' being the local name for the beam that goes across the top of a fireplace. It is over that beam that Chimney Charlie, the resident ghost, spends most of his time, at least when he's not throwing things around. But, nonetheless, the welcome here is a warm and friendly one and the host offers a selection of real ales and a good choice of meals with chicken, red meats, vegetarian, fresh fish from South Devon and shellfood amongst the wide range on offer. This really is a friendly pub, which welcomes well-behaved dogs, children, horses (with a rail for tying them up) and even chickens! One visitor actually arrived with a hen.

Telephone: *01823 421432.*

The **White Hart Inn** at Corfe, a traditional village pub, provides an alternative, serving real ales and a range of meals. In fine weather seating is available outside on the terrace with views across to the Blackdown Hills.

Telephone: *01823 421388.*

 *The Walk*

① From the car park, turn left to head back up to the **B3170**. Turn left and at the next turning left, look for the track which goes off to the right on the opposite side of the road. Head up this track. Ignore the large forestry track leading off to the right and turn left through a gate to reach the corner of a field. Follow the field boundary to a gated entrance into the wood. Follow the track that rises gently towards the crest of **Staple Hill**, which you pass slightly to the left, although it is hidden in the trees. The track then leads downhill to join the lane to **Underhill Farm**.

The trees through which you pass are in ancient woodland with a number of archaeological sites. This was rich hunting territory back in medieval days, when a poacher could lose an eye, or even his life if caught in the act.

Go past **Underhill Farm** and **Bow Green**, ignoring the stile on your left at **Bow Green**.

② About 200 yards past **Bow Green**, turn left through a gate. Head straight across the field to a footbridge. Cross this and keep the same general direction across the next field, keeping the stream on your right-hand side most of the way to reach a metalled road. Turn left onto the road. In about 300 yards, the road bears sharp left to **Staple Park Farm**. Keep straight ahead here into a field. Strictly speaking, the path you need to follow goes diagonally off to the right across the field. You may find it easier to follow the left-hand field boundary along the first side to the corner of the field, turn right, keeping in the field, and then turn right again in the next

corner to reach a gate in about 100 yards.

③ Pass through the gate and follow the track into the woodland straight ahead. The track passes downhill and is joined from the right by a track from **Witch Lodge**. Continue downhill, ignoring the track which doubles back to your left, until the track becomes a tarred lane. Follow this to the metalled road, where you turn left.

④ In ⅓ mile, in the hamlet of **Heale**, turn left onto an obvious

PITMINSTER CHURCH

lane. Follow the track for about 150 yards and then follow the right-hand field boundary to find a footbridge in the corner of the field. Cross this and follow the obvious path leading to **Corfe church**. Turn left onto the B3170 and in about 320 yards, after the houses finish on the right and immediately before the start of a high hedge, turn right into a large field.

The White Hart Inn at Corfe is an old turnpike house and is a traditional village inn serving real ales and good food.

Follow the right-hand field boundary until it disappears to the right. At this point, continue straight ahead, keeping on the track to emerge onto the metalled road which leads into **Pitminster**. Turn right onto the **Pitminster** lane and once in the village, turn left and left again to reach the church.

⑤ Continue past the church and at the end of the track, bear right along the right-hand field boundary to a footbridge. Cross this and continue following the right-hand field boundaries, over footbridges, to reach the metalled road in the village of **Blagdon Hill.**
　　Turn left, going past the **White Lion**, and turn left into **Curdleigh Lane** and then right into **Quarry Lane**. Where the track splits, bend left between the buildings at

Quarry House, following the obvious track uphill into **Prior's Park Wood**.

⑥ At a point where the main track bears left to drop downhill, take the lesser path up to the right. Ignore the next turning to the right and continue straight ahead on the obvious track as it leads uphill and then bears left to a gate at the end of the wood. Continue along the edge of the wood to a gate from where red and white pole markers lead you across a field and through a gate. In about 50 yards, turn right through **Prior's Park Farm** and onto the farm track, which leads down to a B-road.

These woodlands are rich in wildlife. Watch out especially for orchids in the spring and a wealth of fungi in the autumn.

Turn left at the road to reach the **Holman Clavel**, our chosen inn. Care is required along this stretch. Although a minor road, it is straight and fast. Just beyond the inn, bear left to return to the car park.

Date walk completed:

HIGH HAM AND STEMBRIDGE MILL

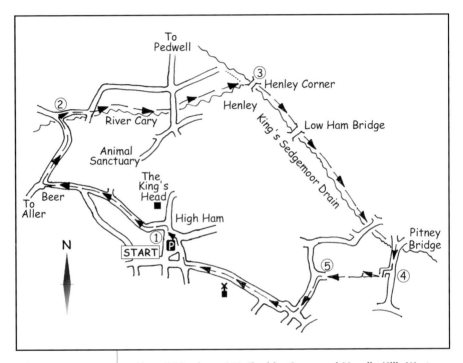

Distance:
6½ miles

Map: OS Explorer 141 Cheddar Gorge and Mendip Hills West

Starting Point:
High Ham village
green.
GR 425311

How to get there: *From the A361 between Street and
Taunton, turn south in the village of Pedwell signposted to
High Ham. In the village centre, park at the village green,
opposite the church.*

*T*he walk begins in the village of High Ham, drops rapidly downhill onto the edge of the low-lying moor and follows the line of the old River Cary and then King's Sedgemoor Drain before heading back uphill to the ridge on which High Ham sits. At the southern edge of the low-lying King's Sedgemoor, this picturesque village stands proud on a crest, from which it enjoys a panoramic view over the moorland below.

It is an ancient parish with a current population of some 800 people, fewer than the thousand or so who lived there a hundred years ago. This perhaps reflects its isolation, being geographically on a road to nowhere. The village green is surrounded by a fine stand of trees and many listed buildings, which include an Elizabethan schoolhouse, not to mention the church, which is quite grand for such a small village. Close by are two hamlets called Beer and Stout, appropriately named as neighbours of Ham.

On the walk you pass Stembridge Tower Mill, and an animal rescue centre, which you may like to visit. On the lower parts of the route, watch out for swans, herons and the occasional bank vole. Below High Ham hill lies the village of Aller, where our chosen inn will be found.

It was at Aller that the Dane Guthrum and his followers were baptised into the Christian faith after being defeated by Alfred the Great (see Walk 9). It is thought that this event may have its parallel in the myth of the Dragon of Aller – where Alfred defeating the Danes is symbolised through the story of John of Aller defeating the dragon. The particular dragon was described as a flying serpent (as on the coat of arms for Somerset). It breathed fire and poisonous fumes and loved fresh milk, frequently attacking milkmaids and sucking cows dry. But John of Aller was made of stern stuff. Having protected himself with a layer of tar (which is the last protection I'd apply if I was about to face a fire-breathing dragon!), he slew the dragon with a nine-foot long spear. This spear is now safely kept at Low Ham church in case another dragon dares to trouble the neighbourhood. An effigy of John of Aller can be found in the village church.

THE OLD POUND INN AT ALLER

 Although the King's Head at High Ham is just yards off the route of this walk, I recommend **The Old Pound Inn**, which is just a mile or so away at Aller, on the A372 Bridgwater to Langport road. It is an old world pub with modern extensions and has twice won the 'Pub of the Year' award. It can also boast the Tourist Board's three stars. There is a huge choice of food with an à la carte menu and bar snacks. Sunday lunch takes some beating.

The Old Pound Inn dates back to 1571 as an inn and cider house. It was extended in 1756 and again in 1980. The beer garden was once a cattle compound, hence 'Old Pound'. Accommodation is available.

Telephone: *01458 250469.*

The Walk

① From the village green, walk past the church and turn left into **Turnhill**

Road. After about 1 mile of almost level walking, you reach the National Trust woodland at **Turnhill**. Continue along the metalled road, dropping downhill rapidly as you bear around to the right, keeping the extensive woodland on the right-hand side. About 200 yards past **Charity Farm**, you reach a T-junction.

② Turn right at the T-junction. Follow this road, with the old **River Cary**, now just a ditch, on your right-hand side. In about ¼ mile, the road turns left, away from the old river. At this point, continue straight ahead, leaving the road through a gateway, and following the ditch until you reach the next road as you approach **Henley**. Cross this road and continue

following the ditch until you reach the **King's Sedgemoor Drain** at **Henley Bridge**.

The King's Sedgemoor Drain is effectively the new River Cary and is part of the critical flood prevention system for the Somerset levels. The riverside stretch between points 2 and 3 is prone to nettle infestation during the summer months. Should this be the case when you take this route, an alternative route can be

STEMBRIDGE MILL

75

found which runs parallel and just to the north, i.e. where the road bears left, follow the road. It then bears right to meet the B-road. At the B-road, go straight across along a drove to the river where you turn right and continue as below.

③ Turn right just before the river and then almost immediately left to cross **Henley Bridge**. Turn right to follow the river, with the river on your right-hand side. After ½ mile, continue straight ahead at **Low Ham Bridge** and again, after a further ¾ mile, at **Broadacre Bridge**. In ¼ mile, turn right over **Pitney Bridge**.

④ In about 250 yards, where the road turns sharp left, pass through a gate on the right-hand side and follow the left-hand field boundary, which soon bears right and then left, into the next field, and then right into a lane. In 200 yards, the lane bears left and, in a further 50 yards, turn right onto a straight drove which

leads back to a metalled road, **Morton's Lane**.

⑤ Turn left onto **Morton's Lane** and, in 500 yards, turn right at the crossroads and then keep straight ahead uphill along the road, which leads to **Stembridge Tower Mill**.

Stembridge Tower Mill is in the ownership of the National Trust and is the nation's last surviving thatched windmill. Built in 1822, it was a working mill up until 1910, capped with a revolving turret and a tail-fin to ensure the blades face into the wind. It is generally open to the public from 2 pm to 5 pm on Sundays and Mondays from April to September. Telephone: 01458 250818 for up-to-date opening hours.

A ¼ mile beyond the mill, turn right. Ignore a turning to the left and keep along this road to a T-junction, where a left turn brings you back to the village green.

 Date walk completed:

HAMBRIDGE AND THE RIVER PARRETT

THE LAMB & LION AT HAMBRIDGE

Distance:
11 miles

Starting Point:
The church in
Hambridge.
GR 393210

Maps: OS Explorer 128 Taunton & Blackdown Hills and
129 Yeovil & Sherborne

How to get there: *Hambridge lies on the B3168 between
Curry Rivel, near Langport, and Ilminster. There is a small
free parking area near the church, or use the Lamb & Lion
car park if consent is sought first.*

77

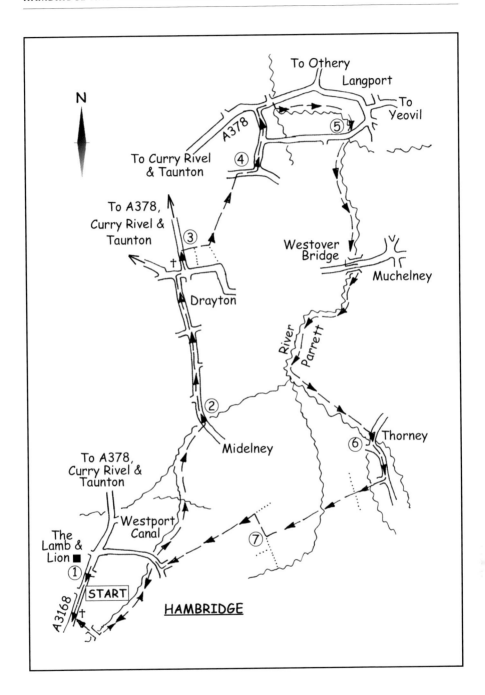

The greater part of this level walk is along riverbanks and canal-side towpaths and crosses through fields where Friesian cattle graze, with swans drifting along the slow-flowing River Parrett. Being so low-lying, the land can be quite sticky after periods of rain but is excellent for walking after a dry spell. Although some 20 miles inland, this whole area is very flat and not far above sea level. Hence winter flooding is common across the district. The village of Muchelney reflects the low-lying moors, its name meaning 'large island'. In fact it is only about 30 ft above sea level. Drainage is a major issue and the moors here are criss-crossed with man-made rhynes and ditches, alongside which run droves to provide access to the fields and convenient routes for walkers. Muchelney is becoming increasingly celebrated as the home of the world-famous potter John Leach, who has a studio in the village. John is the grandson of the Japanese-trained Bernard Leach, considered to be the most influential potter-artist of the 20th century. Bernard's son David continued the tradition and John, the grandson, likewise. His natural ability has led him to create wonderfully inspired and unique pieces. Despite spending an increasing amount of time demonstrating and lecturing in Europe and North America, he has nonetheless found time to create a wildlife reserve next to his studios and has planted over 4,000 hardwood trees and created a pond where he had formerly extracted the clay. It is well worth a visit during this walk.

Watch out for herons, moorhens and lapwing. This part of Somerset is rich in splendid Perpendicular church towers and the one at nearby Huish Episcopi is worth visiting. The walk passes two pubs, the Lamb & Lion at Hambridge and the Drayton Arms in Drayton.

The Walk

① Just south of the church at **Hambridge**, turn left onto the path that runs across the front of the Parish Rooms. Passing a cottage, the path continues between two high hedges. Go through the gate and cross the field, keeping the field boundary to your right. Head straight across the next field to pass through a gap in the hedge to reach the **Westport Canal**. Cross the old footbridge to reach the other bank and turn left.

The Lamb & Lion at Hambridge is a 16th century inn, which, within living memory, was combined with a farm and slaughterhouse. It has a friendly atmosphere with its open bar and timbered ceilings and offers the usual range of real ales plus an à la carte menu and list of daily specials. The inn is apparently named after a local vicar who entered the inn 'like a lion and left like a lamb', rather worse for wear. There is a large parking area at the front of the inn, which is occasionally used by local Morris dancing teams. Walkers can park here if consent is first sought. There is also seating in the garden area.

Telephone: *01460 281355.*

Follow the towpath, crossing the road that runs from **Hambridge** to **Stembridge**, until reaching the next road, which runs between **Drayton** and **Midelney** (pronounced Midney).

Midelney Manor was the ancient home of the Abbots of Muchelney, although the house that stands today is of Elizabethan origin. Within the grounds is a rarely seen falcons' mews.

② Turn left onto this road to head into the village of **Drayton**. On reaching a T-junction, turn right. You will find the church on your left and the **Drayton Arms** on your right. Turn left immediately after the church, into **North Street**.

The Drayton Arms offers an alternative watering hole and has indoor and outdoor seating.

③ In a short distance, you will come to **Northover Farm** on your right. Immediately after the farm barn, turn right. A signpost on the barn wall shows this to be the footpath to 'Langport 1 mile'. At the end of the short green track, enter into the field and head for the stile almost straight across in front of you. Ignore the finger sign pointing to a footpath to the right.

Immediately after crossing the stile, turn left to enter a short area of scrub. In a short distance, you will emerge into an open field. Turn right here and follow the footpath, keeping the hedge on your right. On reaching the corner of the field, pass through a small gap in the hedge to emerge into the next field.

Before you, as though in the middle of the field, you will see a small woodland. To its right is the church tower of **Langport**. You will

A FISHERMAN ON THE RIVER PARRETT AT MUCHELNEY

also see three telegraph poles in the field in front of you. The middlemost of these will be at the left-hand edge of the woodland. Head for this pole, at the base of which you will find another small gap in the hedge, which takes you into the next field.

Follow the footpath, keeping the trees on your right until you reach the end of the woodland. The next bit can be tricky, since the footpath is not always clear, thanks to crop planting. It may therefore be necessary to follow the field boundary round to your destination on the far side of the field.

Before you and slightly to your left will be seen **Merrick's Farm**, a cream-coloured building. This is on a track which leads across in front of it. Further along that track to the right is a willow grower's cottage, where withy canes can often be seen standing. There are also two poles about 12 ft high with a bar going across the top. This is in the withy grower's yard and it is there that you will find the stile to take you onto the gravel road.

Head diagonally across the field to this stile, or around the field margins if crops dictate.

④ On reaching the lane, turn right and follow the road as it bears left, leading up into **Frog Lane** and to the main road in **Langport**.

Turn right at the main road and, after crossing the river bridge, turn right following the riverside footpath, with the river on your right.

Along here can be seen the fine church towers of Langport, on your left, and Huish Episcopi. A number of towers become visible along this walk and between them represent some of the finest Perpendicular church towers in the county.

⑤ In just over ½ mile, you reach a small gravel car park where the concrete **Huish Bridge** crosses the river. Cross over this bridge and turn left to once again follow the riverbank, but this time keeping it to your left-hand side.

Here the low-lying fields are divided by large ditches. After floods in winter they offer a suitable habitat for many wading birds and at times large flocks of tumbling lapwing can be seen.

Continue along the river to **Westover Bridge**. Here cross the bridge to continue your riverbank walk but now on the other bank, with the river on your left-hand side.

At Westover Bridge, you may like to take a diversion into Muchelney to visit the ancient abbey, with a very pleasant tearoom just opposite. Also in the village are the workshops of John Leach, the internationally famous potter.

Follow the riverbank all the way to the road, which runs south from **Muchelney** through the village of **Thorney**.

⑥ Turn right onto this metalled road and in ¼ mile turn right onto a long, straight drove.

Thorney is a small village with a mixture of red brick, stone and whitewashed houses, some thatched. It is in Thorney that the annual Lowland Games are held each year with such events as 'welly' throwing, terrier racing, raft racing and even mud wrestling.

Follow this straight track for 1 mile, crossing a drove and a river bridge on the way to reach a T-junction.

(7) Turn right here and then left at the next T-junction in about 300 yards.

In about ¾ mile, on reaching the metalled road, turn right and in a short distance just before the bridge over the **Westport Canal**, turn left to retrace your steps along the towpath and back to the church.

The Westport Canal was built in the mid 19th century and saw active service for some 40 years or so. Connecting to the River Parrett, it was the tail end of a link to the Bristol Channel with access also to Taunton and nearby Langport. It closed in 1878 and survives remarkably well.

Date walk completed:

ILCHESTER AND CHILTON CANTELO

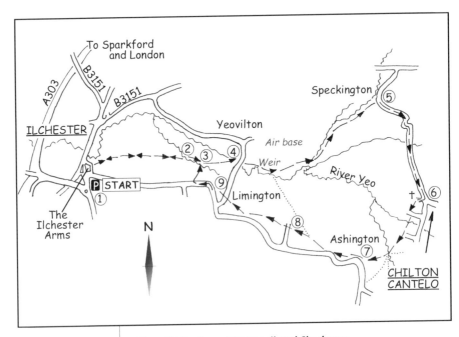

Distance:
8 miles

Map: OS Explorer 129 Yeovil and Sherborne

Starting Point:
Free car park near Ilchester Town Hall, at the junction of Church Street and Limington Road. GR 523225

How to get there: *From the A303, take the A37 road to Yeovil. In ½ mile, turn left into Ilchester. The Town Hall is on your left and free parking on the right as you enter the village.*

THE ILCHESTER ARMS

*T*his is an easy, level walk around the meandering rivers Yeo and Cam. It is predominantly through dairy pasture and arable land with just one stretch of road walking, albeit almost traffic free. Life around Ilchester and Chilton Cantelo is dominated by the RNAS Yeovilton site. Ilchester's presence as a service base dates back 2,000 years when it was *Londinis*, a Roman military base on the Fosse Way. Apart from the ever-present helicopters, you may spot herons, kingfishers and plenty of roe deer. Chilton Cantelo takes its name from the Cantilupe family. The village is perhaps best known for the 'Screaming Skull'. Theophilus Broome, a staunch Parliamentarian who died in 1670, feared that on his death, the Royalists would display his head on a spear. To avoid such reprisals, he left instructions for his skull to be kept at Higher Farm – where it allegedly screams if anyone tries to move it!

The Ilchester Arms, first licensed in 1686, is a charming building full of character. Originally known as the George and then the Swan, it became a draper's shop in 1894 until destroyed by fire in 1925. In 1995 it became the Ilchester Arms and today offers British cuisine using local produce. The hotel boasts a bar where bar snacks are served (soups, ploughman's, pasta, chicken dishes, salads), a restaurant (a range of meat, seafood and vegetarian dishes) and, for the summer months, seating in the pleasant gardens, where dogs are welcome. Overnight en-suite accommodation is available.

Telephone: *01935 840220.*

The Walk

① On leaving the car park, turn right and immediately left into **Free Street**. Go straight ahead between two walls to cross concrete steps and turn immediately right through a kissing gate. Follow the signposted footpath as you pass the **River Yeo** on your left and then follow the left-hand field boundary, ignoring a gate along the way, to reach a waymarked stile in the field corner.

Cross the stile and follow the left-hand field boundary to cross a stile and footbridge into the next field. Now head for the far left corner, where you cross the top end of a track to enter the next field. Head slightly to your left, uphill, to reach a hedge which you follow, keeping it to your right. Cross a stile into the next field and maintain the same direction to reach the far corner of that field and cross a stile on the right-hand side of a gate. Bear left to cross the stream, using a footbridge.

② Turn right, keeping the stream on your right-hand side. Cross a footbridge over a sluice, still following the stream, to reach a small wooden gate. (There will now be a footbridge to your right to cross over the stream. Ignore this for the time being but you will cross this on your return route to retrace your steps from here.)

③ Pass through the gate and head slightly left towards the right of the high radar scanner and pass through a field gate into a second field. Maintain the same direction, heading just to the right of the road bridge to emerge onto the road.

④ Turn left, cross over the bridge and bear right.

There is an attractive weir here and the presence of a garden bench makes it an ideal spot for a picnic break. It is also an alternative place to park and start the walk. It provides a useful fishing spot as well and good-sized chub are often taken here at the base of the weir.

Just before the first house on the right, turn right to enter a riverside field through a V-stile and go straight ahead along the waymarked route to pass just to the left of a row of lights on high poles.

These are used as direction markers for aircraft on the nearby air base.

Cross into the next field and head for the top right corner. Ignore the footbridge to the right but pass through the gate in front of you, after which turn left to follow the left-hand field boundary.

For the next section of the walk you will be following one edge of the Royal Naval Air Base at Yeovilton. Helicopters and jump jets will be active almost continuously and it is amazing how the cattle and sheep simply ignore all the activity. RNAS Yeovilton, also known as HMS Heron, is one of the country's two active Fleet Air Arm bases and is home to the Navy's Lynx helicopters and the Royal Marines' Westland Sea

Kings. Until April 2006, it was also home to the Harrier jump-jets, which can be quite deafening on take-off. The site covers a total of 4 square kilometres and is manned by around 1,700 service personnel and 2,000 civilians. It was established more than 60 years ago and now has very strong links with the local communities. During those years, the runways have been extended, allowing training for those pilots who, one day, will take off from aircraft carriers or who will enter enemy territory using their vertical take off and landing capabilities. Most of the activity you will witness as you circumnavigate the base will involve helicopters. Please remember that it is a military base and that warnings about not entering should be taken seriously.

Having said that, visitors are more than welcome to the Fleet Air Arm Museum which is on the site and is well worth a visit, especially for those with children. It contains a wealth of aircraft from the two world wars and the Falklands conflict. Also there is a mock up of HMS Ark Royal as she was in the 1970s and this attraction offers the benefit of a simulated helicopter flight! (Telephone 01935 840565 for details.)

At the end of the footpath, turn right through a gate and cross the

THE WEIR AT YEOVILTON VILLAGE

River Cam, using the footbridge. Turn left to follow the small river. Pass through a gate and continue along the left-hand field boundary. At the end of the airfield, the river bends to the right, away from the air station. Shortly after this, ignore the river bridge on your left. Instead continue along the left-hand field boundary, past a 6ft-high pile of rocks, to pass through a gate into the next field, where you continue along the left-hand field boundary. On reaching a stone bridge, bear right across the field towards a set of gates.

⑤ Pass through the pedestrian gate to emerge onto a road. Turn right and follow the road into the village of **Chilton Cantelo**, turning right at the crossroads at **Old School House**.

⑥ Immediately before the church, turn left onto a signposted footpath to '**Ashington** 1m'. Follow the path, with a high wall on your right, to cross another path, where you continue straight ahead between hedgerows to reach a road. Turn right and in 20 yards turn left onto a signposted footpath over a stile, to follow a narrow track between hedgerows.

On your right is Chilton Cantelo School, an independent school with almost 400 pupils. The main building was an 18th century manor house.

At the end of the path, cross a stile, a footbridge and another stile to enter a field. Once in the field, head slightly left, keeping to the left of the double telegraph pole where a gate allows you to cross a bridge over the **River Yeo**. Follow the right-hand field boundary to reach a road, ignoring the track to the right.

⑦ Turn right onto the road to pass through **Ashington** village. After the church and **Manor Cottage**, enter the first field on the right by crossing the stile and head diagonally left across the field to emerge back on the road in the opposite corner. In 100 yards, after a left-hand bend, take the second gate on the right, waymarked and signposted to 'Limington 1¼ m'. Head half-left across the field to cross a footbridge over a ditch. Keep the same line of direction to reach a field gate opposite.

Pass through the waymarked gate and follow the left-hand field boundary. In the next field bear slightly right (or follow the right-hand field boundary if crops dictate that you are unable to follow the official path), to cross a simple plank footbridge over a ditch onto a drove.

⑧ Go straight across the drove, over a waymarked stile and then head diagonally right, just to the right of the nearest telegraph pole, to cross a stile in the right-hand field boundary. Cross the double stile and turn left to follow the left-hand field boundary to cross the next double stile and plank bridge into the next

field. Follow the left-hand field boundary, heading towards a group of houses.

Cross another double stile and the next field, heading just to the left of a large tree which is well to the right of the houses. In the next field, head diagonally right towards the opposite corner to reach a gate onto a road.

⑨ Turn right onto the road and in 20 yards turn left onto a signposted footpath to '**Limington church** ¼ m'. Head for the right-hand corner of the field to pass through a V-stile. Turn right to enter the churchyard and follow the path as it bears left to reach the road.

Turn right and follow the road round a left-hand bend. Opposite '**Hillside**' turn right, over a stile, onto a waymarked footpath. Follow the right-hand field boundary, through a gate, into the next field where you continue along the right-hand field boundary to reach a stile in the corner. Cross this and the plank bridge. Turn left to cross a footbridge over the river.

This gets you back to point 3 on your outward journey. Turn left here to retrace your steps back to **Ilchester**.

Date walk completed:

CADBURY CASTLE AND CORTON DENHAM

THE CAMELOT INN AT SOUTH CADBURY

Distance:
8¼ miles

Starting Point:
South Cadbury
village free car
park.
GR 632253

Map: OS Explorer 129 Yeovil and Sherborne

How to get there: *From the A303 between Ilchester
and Wincanton, turn south, signposted South Cadbury.
In ½ mile, enter the village and follow the car park signs.
After passing the Camelot inn and the church, which
will be on your right, the car park is on the left.*

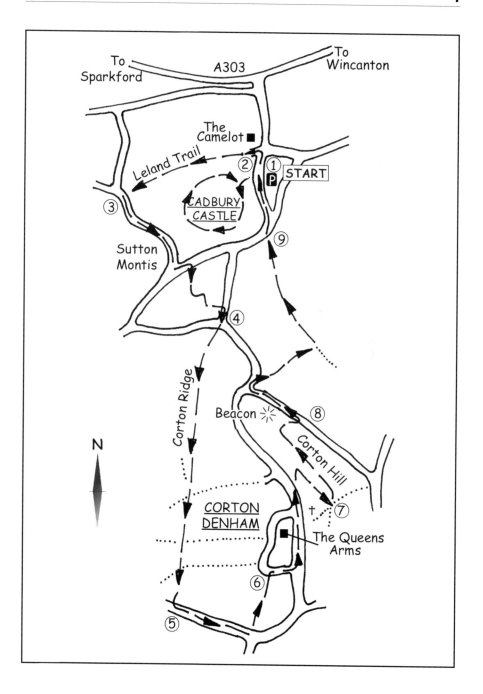

*T*his walk offers stunning views across Somerset and Dorset as it follows the Corton Ridge and the escarpment of Corton Hill, with a well justified detour at the start of the walk to take in mystical Cadbury Castle. This is the land of King Arthur and local legend has it that it was at Cadbury Castle that Arthur died and from there was taken by three queens across the Somerset Levels to Glastonbury, where his remains were laid to rest. Picture this as you stand atop Cadbury Castle or take a rest at the Beacon on Corton Hill, from where you can visualise the route they trod. On stretches of the walk, the Fleet Air Arm base at Yeovilton can be clearly seen with its illuminated runways and provides a striking contrast with those images of the court of King Arthur – latter day and present day guardians of our nation. The Queen's Arms in Corton Denham offers an alternative pub stop and has a bar for walkers.

The Camelot inn at South Cadbury is a free house with a light and airy bar plus the benefit of a beer garden. It has been recognised by Les Routiers and appears in the *2006 Which Good Food Guide*. Ample parking is available behind the inn. The food is very good with a range of bar snacks, an à la carte menu and real ales.

There is an interesting collection of archaeological material on display, fitting in well with the history which goes with the village. Indeed, the castle hill at South Cadbury had been a military stronghold for four millennia. It was once the home of the Durotriges tribe, from whose name Dorset is derived, and this walk is right on Dorset's border, one section actually treading the boundary.

Well-behaved dogs are welcome. There is no accommodation at the inn but bed and breakfast is available nearby.

Telephone: *01963 440448.*

 *The Walk*

① Leaving the car park, turn right to head back towards the church. The first part of the walk is an exploration of **Cadbury Castle**. Just after the first house on the left, turn left to head up **Castle Lane**. After going through a gate, the path dips down as you pass through the wooded area of the lower rampart. In a short distance, take the path to the left, which brings you to a water trough and an arch-covered bowl known as 'King Arthur's Well'. Continue along the path, which bears right round the hill fort. Almost halfway round, the path forks. Take the lower path through a wood, continuing around the hill, past 'Queen Anne's Wishing Well', to return to the access lane. Now turn right to find the centre of the hill fort

before retracing your steps down the access route and back to the road.

Cadbury Castle was an immense Iron Age fortification, the second largest in the country. In places the ramparts are 40 ft high. Around 1,500 years ago, at the time of King Arthur, there was a considerable community here. After the Romans had left our shores, there were numerous battles between the Celts and

VIEW FROM HIGH UP ON CADBURY CASTLE

Saxons. *Cadbury Castle was an ideal site for a leader such as King Arthur. Could this be Arthur's Camelot? Modern opinion is that it is indeed the site of Arthur's court. As a fortified hill fort it was massive. Certainly the locals are convinced, for, when a recent archaeological excavation was commenced, an aged local asked if they had come to remove the king's remains. On that excavation they discovered that the ramparts had been strengthened with large amounts of masonry from old Roman buildings, and that raised walkways had been created. In one corner, there was a cobbled road passing through a significant wooden gatehouse. A meeting hall more than 20 metres by 10 was uncovered and pottery, befitting the status of a king, dated this all back to the 5th century AD.*

② At the road, turn left and then left again after the church, turning into **Folly Lane**, where the **Camelot inn** is on the corner. Follow this lane as it turns to a dirt track.

You will now be following the Leland Trail, which is reasonably well signposted, until you reach the next road.

At the end of the track, cross a stile on your right into a field. Turn left and follow the left-hand field boundary for four fields to reach a stile on your left. Cross this and turn right to follow the right-hand field boundary to reach a lane.

③ Turn left on the lane to enter the village of **Sutton Montis**. Go past the church and take the road to the left. In about 200 yards, turn right onto a farm track between hedgerows. Follow this as it turns left, right and then left to reach a proper road.

④ Turn right on the road to reach a T-junction. At the T-junction, go straight across the road onto a bridleway (**The Monarch's Way**) heading south-west. It bears right and then left as it passes round the right-hand side of **Parrock Hill**. The sunken track turns to a less obvious track as it passes along the crest of **Corton Ridge**. To your left you can see the village of **Corton Denham**, which you will pass through on your return route. Ignore the various paths off to the left, which lead down to the village, until you come to a T-junction as your path begins a slow descent.

⑤ Turn left at the T-junction (**Windmill Hill**) and follow this track downhill towards the road at **Stafford's Green**. Before the road is a farm. Turn left at the farm just before a stream, following the left-hand field boundary with the stream to your right. Enter the next field and continue straight ahead, heading slightly to the left of the church tower, to reach a road.

(6) Turn right onto the road and then left at the T-junction. Go past the **Queen's Arms** on your left to reach the far end of **Corton Denham** village. Opposite the **Post Office Stores** on the left, turn right onto a track that leads uphill. In about 120 yards, the track splits. Take the path to the right which doubles back to continue up **Corton Hill** along an obvious track.

(7) On reaching a private road, without entering the road, double back again, this time to the left and uphill, to follow a path along the top edge of the escarpment following the right-hand field boundary. Pass through two long fields in this way. Approaching the end of the second large field, the boundary takes a turn to the right and in a short distance you enter a third field. By following this field boundary as it turns right, you reach the road.

But first, before taking to the road, head for the obvious beacon, the highest point on Corton Ridge,

which is about 150 yards away. A stone bench awaits you, along with super views. The nearby hill is Parrock Hill, which you passed earlier on the other side. The obvious shape of Glastonbury Tor is easy to identify. To the right of the tor are the Mendip Hills and to the left the Quantock Hills and, further left again, the Brendons.

(8) At the road, turn left to head steeply downhill to a T-junction. Turn right and almost immediately right again along the lane to **Whitcombe**. Follow this lane for about ⅓ mile as it turns into a track between hedgerows. At the end of the track, turn left to walk along the hillside, following the right-hand field boundary. After crossing two fields and stiles, you reach a farm lane. A short distance along this lane is a barn, at a point where the lane turns left. Continue straight ahead here to cross a stream using a footbridge and reach the metalled road.

(9) Turn right onto the road and almost immediately bear left at the fork to return to your car park and the **Camelot inn**.

Date walk completed:

YARLINGTON AND CASTLE CARY

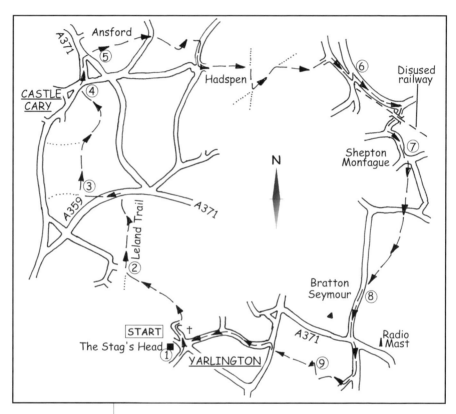

Distance:
11 miles

Starting Point:
Off-road free
parking area
between Yarlington
church and the
Stag's Head.
GR 654293

Map: OS Explorer 142 Shepton Mallet and Mendip Hills East

How to get there: *From the A303 between Ilchester and
Wincanton, turn north, signposted North Cadbury, and
follow the road for 1¼ miles. Turn left, signposted
'Yarlington ½ mile'. In the centre of the village, turn left at
the T-junction to park between the church and the inn.*

*T*his route explores the low hills of South Somerset – quite unlike those of the Mendips and Exmoor, these are gentler, more curving, more pastoral. Starting at Yarlington, the walk heads north, taking advantage of the Leland Trail, to reach Castle Cary. This part of South Somerset provides pleasant walking with buildings of considerable interest. Yarlington House with its Tuscan columns and Venetian windows dates back to 1790. Castle Cary has a very pleasant atmosphere with its honey-coloured stone houses, many of which are fine examples of Georgian architecture. The golden colour stone comes from nearby Ham quarry. Castle Cary's earlier wealth was built on textiles, cloth being produced from the 14th century onwards and today John Boyd Textiles, established in 1837, survives as the only horse-hair weaving factory in the country.

Dominating the town centre is the Market House, which accommodates the town's museum, complete with two prison cells and an information centre. Behind the Market House is Bailey Hill, where a pepper-pot prison lock-up will be found. This dates back to the 18th century and is one of only four such examples in the country. The town is also blessed with an interesting range of shops and eating houses. Keep an eye open for the remains of the keep of the Norman castle, which the walk passes as it enters this old town.

The **Stag's Head** at Yarlington is a traditional small village pub; no fruit machines, no pool tables, but a good choice of bar snacks and more substantial meals. There is also a wide selection of real ales, wines and spirits and the pub was recommended in the *Good Beer Guide*. There is even a dog menu! It is a 'talking pub' with a friendly host and a beer garden, where a stream runs alongside. Food is served from 12 noon to 2 pm and 7 pm to 9 pm in the evenings. It is an inn that lends itself to walkers, where I found a friendly welcome.

Telephone: *01963 440393.*

THE STAG'S HEAD AT YARLINGTON

 *The Walk*

ground on stones to keep the grain dry and away from vermin.

① Standing with your back to the **Stag's Head** in **Yarlington**, turn left and then almost immediately right into the lane which leads to **Manor Farm**, passing the church on your right. On reaching the farm, turn right through the farmyard.

To your right is an interesting granary store, raised above the

Follow the concrete track to its end at a gate. Turn right onto a short lane with two gates at the end. Take the left-hand gate and follow the bridleway with the steep side of the valley immediately on your right. The path bears gradually to the left. About ¾ mile after the farm, the **Leland Trail/Monarch's Way** (**Hick's Lane**) cuts across your path.

② Turn right onto the track to head north along the **Leland Trail**, following the track and field boundary and passing a ruined windmill, to reach the main road, the A359. After crossing the stile onto the road, turn left.

In 200 yards, on reaching an electricity transformer, turn right, signposted **Coopers Ash Lane**, and follow the right-hand field boundary to reach the corner of the field.

③ Cross the stile into the next field and follow the yellow marker by turning right and keeping to the right-hand field boundary, heading towards a radio mast. At the end of the field, cross over to continue through the next field, following the left-hand field boundary and passing an enclosed reservoir and trig point. In the bottom corner of the field, an obvious track leads you down to the centre of **Castle Cary**.

④ On reaching **Fore Street**, turn right and proceed into the **High Street** and then left into **Ansford Road**. At the end of **Ansford Road**, turn right onto the main road (A371) and in about 50 yards, turn left by **Ansford Farm House** into **Solomon's Lane**.

Ansford was the birthplace in 1740 of the diarist Parson Woodforde, who recorded the social life in this rural community during the 1770s when he served here as the curate.

His diaries provide a fascinating insight into the place and the period.

⑤ Follow this lane as it climbs uphill, signposted **Hadspen**, following the **Leland Trail** and ignoring a bold track off to your left, to reach the **Wyke Road**. At the road, turn left and in about 50 yards turn right through a gate by an old quarry. This takes you into **Knap Hollow**, a cleft valley leading downhill and no longer on the **Leland Trail**. Follow this bridleway, keeping to the hedge on your left. At the bottom of the descent, by a disused pit, pass through a gate, following the obvious path as it bears left around a stand of trees.

This stand of coppiced trees was probably the source of fuel for the owners of the pit, used to smelt lime for use on the land as fertilizer.

Continue along this obvious track as it bears right to ascend to the metalled road, where you turn right to head into the hamlet of **Hadspen**. About 25 yards past a post box, turn left into the **Nettlecombe Hill** lane, a partly cobbled sunken track. At the end of the track, you reach a T-junction. Turn right to a crossroad of tracks and there turn left, heading towards **Pitcombe**. In about 150 yards, after passing a ruined barn, turn right by a rickety gate, across a

THE ANCIENT LOCK-UP AT CASTLE CARY

stile to drop down into a combe, heading towards a pair of pine trees, which will lead you to a stile in the hedge.

Cross the stile and follow the lane down past the church and on to the T-junction. Turn right and follow the road all the way down to the main **A359**.

⑥ At the main road, turn sharp left and in a short distance sharp right, heading towards **The Towers**. In ½ mile, turn right and follow the road across the disused railway line, to reach a T-junction. Turn left and follow the road past the church and to a point where the road splits at **Lower Farm**.

⑦ Take the left-hand path and in a short distance turn right over a stile and continue straight ahead, in a southerly direction across the field, eventually picking up the left-hand field boundary. Follow this to the corner of the field. Turn left across a stile and then turn right to reach the corner of the next field, where you cross a double stile at a cattle trough.

In the next field, continue south by heading diagonally across the field, using a radio mast on the horizon as a marker. Two cottages will become visible before you. Head directly for these and on reaching the road, turn right along the road for about 40 yards and then turn left onto the signposted footpath, into a garden,

across a paddock and over a railway sleeper footbridge crossing a stream. Once across, go straight ahead, keeping to the middle of the roughly triangular-shaped field before you and heading for the apex of the triangle and just to the right of a radio mast in front of you.

At the top of the field, cross a double stile and a stream to head uphill through the next field towards a grey house. Enter the next field through a gate and head diagonally left, continuing uphill, to enter a green lane. Once in the lane, turn right to cross a paddock towards **Church Farm**. Pass through the farm to reach the road.

⑧ At the road, turn left, passing through the village of **Bratton Seymour**, to reach the main **A371** road.

The junction at the main road is popularly known as Jack White's Gibbet, the site of the hanging of a murderer by that name. There is many a spooky story linked with this place, where passers-by report hearing his ghostly voice.

Turn left and almost immediately right on the **Holton** road. In ⅓ mile, turn right onto a drive alongside a bungalow. Continue along the drive to reach a cattle grid just before **New Park Farm**. Turn right before the grid, cross a stile, turn right again through a hunting gate and then go straight ahead to pass through a gateway into the next field. Follow the left-hand field boundary downhill towards the woods. In the next field follow the right-hand field boundary and then turn right to pass through a gated gap between two areas of woodland.

⑨ Bear left to follow the right-hand edge of the wood to its end, from which point you follow the stream down to the road. Turn right at the road and in 100 yards turn left to follow the road into the village of **Yarlington** and back to the **Stag's Head**.

 Date walk completed:

GLASTONBURY AND WEST PENNARD

THE LION AT PENNARD

Distance: 7 miles	Map: OS Explorer 141 Cheddar Gorge and Mendip Hills West
Starting Point: The car park of the Lion at Pennard, at West Pennard. GR 547386	**How to get there:** *3 miles east of Glastonbury on the A361 to Shepton Mallet, the Lion at Pennard is easily spotted alongside the main road. Patrons are welcome to use the pub car park whilst walking. Otherwise use roadside parking away from the A361.*

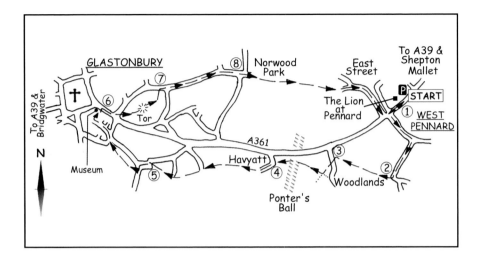

Although about 20 miles inland, you begin this walk at just a few feet above sea level, and ascend to the tip of Glastonbury Tor. En route you pass the Rural Life Museum, which is well recommended as a mid-point diversion. There are wonderful vistas in all directions and from Glastonbury Tor the views are stunning. Glastonbury is a spiritual centre for many and the county's most famous landmark for others. The town is full of fascinating shops that offer alternative medicines and religions, and bookshops that reflect this culture. There are probably more 'vegetarian' offerings per acre here than in any other tourist town in the country! The abbey grounds are just off the route and can easily be visited with a small diversion. West Pennard has a number of houses with 16th century origins and a church that dates back to the 15th century.

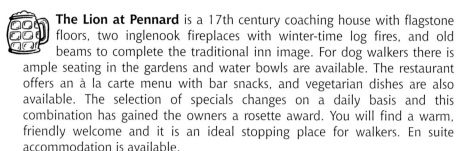

The Lion at Pennard is a 17th century coaching house with flagstone floors, two inglenook fireplaces with winter-time log fires, and old beams to complete the traditional inn image. For dog walkers there is ample seating in the gardens and water bowls are available. The restaurant offers an à la carte menu with bar snacks, and vegetarian dishes are also available. The selection of specials changes on a daily basis and this combination has gained the owners a rosette award. You will find a warm, friendly welcome and it is an ideal stopping place for walkers. En suite accommodation is available.

Telephone: *01458 832941.*

The Walk

① From the **Lion**, head along the A361 towards **Glastonbury** and in about 100 yards turn left, signposted to **West Bradley**. In 600 yards the road bears right and, in another 500 yards, it bears sharp left.

② At this bend, turn right through the second gate. Follow the right-hand field boundary towards **Glastonbury Tor** to pass through a gate to the left of three isolated trees. Follow the left-hand field boundary to its end, where you turn right, following the hedge line until, just after a bend in the hedge, you turn left over a footbridge, which is usually hidden in the hedge. Cross this and continue heading towards the Tor until you reach a metalled road. Turn left onto the road and continue to **Woodlands Farm**.

③ Turn right at the farm onto the farm lane, between barns, going through a gate as the lane bears right towards the farm. Now head south-west along the right-hand field boundary with its deep ditch. In 150 yards after the farm, turn right to cross a stile, after which you walk parallel to the left-hand field boundary, heading just to the left of the Tor, to pass into the next field. Beyond you can clearly see the high embankment that is **Ponter's Ball**.

Ponter's Ball is an Iron Age embankment and runs for ¾ mile, roughly north to south.

Just after a water trough, cross a stone stile to climb the embankment, keeping your line of direction. From the top of the embankment, keep to the same general direction, heading just left of the red-roofed house, to cross a stile and footbridge. Continue by heading for the white bungalow, to cross another stile, which leads onto a farm lane.

④ Turn left onto the lane and follow it around a bend to where it finishes at two field gates. Take the right-hand of these, signposted 'Cinnamon Lane 1¼ m', to enter an orchard. Head across the orchard to the diagonally opposite corner to cross a stile to the next field. Follow the right-hand field boundary for the next two fields to reach a farm lane. Turn left, keeping the farm and dairy on your right, crossing a stile and heading for the right-hand end of a stand of trees, complete with rookery. Pass through a wooden gate and head towards the white house immediately ahead.

⑤ Cross the tarmac area at the large house to cross a stile, staying to the left of the tennis courts. Follow the right-hand field boundary, keeping to the distinct path until you reach the metalled road at Cinnamon Lane, at Lower Edgarley, where you continue in the same general direction along the road. Follow this road, turning left onto the Coxbridge road and in 100 yards turn right, over a stile, to follow the right-hand field boundary until its end at a housing estate. Cross the stile onto the estate, turn right to go

uphill along Challice Way. Keep to Challice Way until you have passed Bilbary Lane and Hood Close on the right-hand side. On reaching railings opposite the Actis Road nameplate, turn right to enter the car park of the Glastonbury Rural Life Museum.

The Rural Life Museum, with free admission, really is well worth a visit. Children will especially enjoy it with the sheep and chickens free ranging in the small orchard. You can also enjoy light refreshments on their patio area. The medieval Abbey Barn contains a wonderful collection of old farm wagons.

Continue straight through the car park, going to the left of a small hut raised off the ground on staddle-stones, and follow the short path up to the main road, Chilkwell Street.

⑥ Cross the road and turn right. Just after the Chalice Well Gardens, turn left into Well House Lane, past a cattle grid, and then immediately right to follow a well-marked path to the top of Glastonbury Tor.

The Chalice Well which lies at the foot of the Tor is claimed to be the place where Joseph of Arimathea buried the Holy Grail, the chalice cup which contained the blood of Christ. Joseph was Christ's maternal great uncle and provided the tomb for his nephew's burial. Carrying the Holy Grail, which contained the blood and sweat of Christ, he travelled with St Philip on an evangelical tour of France. Philip sent him to Britain, where he was familiar with Somerset from his days as a trader. On stopping at Glastonbury, he stuck his staff, made from the tree which provided the crown of thorns at Christ's crucifixion, into the ground and it took root. Every year, at Christmas, a sprig of blossom is cut from Glastonbury's Holy Thorn and sent to the royal family.

Glastonbury Tor is an icon of Somerset and the views from the top are spectacular. An interpretation panel indicates all the landmarks around the area and the ruins of St Michael's Chapel offer welcome shade on a hot day, with stone benches inside. It was here that Henry VIII had Abbot Richard Whiting hung,

THE ABBEY BARN AT GLASTONBURY

drawn and quartered for refusing to conform to the new rules on worship after the break with Catholicism.

Having taken in the views from the top, descend the Tor on the opposite side, following the distinct path, over a stile, past a sheep dip on the left, to reach a metalled road, **Stone Down Lane**.

⑦ Turn right onto the road, ignoring the turning right in 100 yards, and continue along this road as it becomes a lane, eventually reaching a metalled road again at **Norwood Park**.

⑧ Go straight across at the road, over a gravel area, to reach a gate on the left-hand side of the courtyard. Pass through the gate and turn immediately right to go over a stile

in the corner of a small field. Keeping to the left of the farm buildings, follow the concrete farm track downhill towards **East Street**.

There are particularly fine views along the next stretch. Behind you is the Tor, to the left are the Mendips, ahead is Pennard Hill.

At the end of the farm lane, cross a stile and continue in the same direction, ignoring the stile on your left by a water trough. Continue ahead, crossing a number of stiles, a footbridge and further stiles that mark the way to a farm lane at **East Street Farm**. Follow the farm track, keeping the farm to your right, as it becomes a metalled road leading down to the A39. At the main road, turn left to return to the **Lion at Pennard**.

Date walk completed:

WRINGTON AND CONGRESBURY

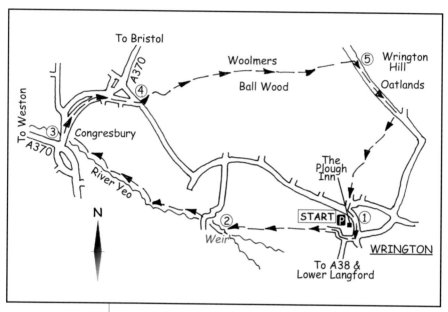

Distance:
7 miles

Starting Point:
The Plough Inn at
Wrington.
GR 469629

Map: OS Explorer 154 Bristol West and Portishead,
Congresbury and Chew Magna

How to get there: From the A38, just north of Churchill,
take the B3133 through Lower Langford and on to
Wrington. Entering Wrington, pass along Station Road,
bearing right into Broad Street and then left into the High
Street for the Plough Inn. There is also ample kerb-side
parking in the centre of the village.

THE BEER GARDEN OF THE PLOUGH INN WITH ITS PETANQUE PITCH

*T*his is a pleasant walk in the valley of the River Yeo, through woodland in one direction balanced with pastoral riverside walking in the other, following the Two Rivers Way. Wrington's best known former resident is Hannah More, whose thatched cottage is at Barley Wood. Hannah More was a poet, playwright and the founder of many schools in the Mendip area during the 18th century. She was also the founder of female friendly societies set up to help the sick and poor. A staunch Christian, Hannah and her sisters are buried in Wrington churchyard. The nearby Waterpool Farm has a chambered long barrow. Although the chosen inn is in Wrington, Congresbury offers a number of alternatives, such as the Ship and Castle in the High Street, where public toilets are sited in the car park, and Paddington's Café in Broad Street.

The Plough Inn will be found in Wrington's High Street, in the centre of this affluent village. Apart from a patio area, it has a huge garden and dogs are welcome both inside and out. A wide choice of meals and ales is on offer in this rustically comfortable country pub, which has proved very popular with the walking fraternity. There is a large car park and patrons are welcome to leave their cars here whilst walking.

Telephone: *01934 862871.*

The Walk

① From the **Plough Inn**, turn right into **Broad Street**. As **Broad Street** bears left, go straight ahead into **The Triangle** and then right to enter **Ladywell**. In 50 yards, turn right onto a signposted footpath (not the 'Private Drive') to follow a path through a kissing-gate into a field. Turn left and follow the left-hand field boundary until the hedge turns left, away from you, and continue straight ahead to reach a stile in the hedge opposite. In the next field, follow the right-hand field boundary to a stile at the next corner. Cross this, turn left to cross another stile and follow the left-hand field boundary, maintaining your previous line of travel.

After passing under overhead power lines, turn left over a stile, then turn right to follow the right-hand field boundary. Cross a stile alongside a gate into the next field and then turn half-left to cross the field. Ignore the gate on your right but take the gate ahead of you to follow the right-hand field boundary to a stile. Cross this and turn left through the next field to reach a footbridge over the River Yeo.

② Cross the footbridge and turn right to follow the river bank. On reaching the road, turn right to cross the river again, this time turning left to follow the river on the other bank all the way to **Congresbury**.

At Congresbury, the church is worth a visit with its wagon-vaulted roof on stone corbels displaying carvings of small men wearing red and green, their faces swollen as if suffering from double mumps. Legend has it that St Congar arrived here when fleeing his father, the King of Cornwall. Having dreamt of a wild boar asleep in the bushes, he decided to stay and planted his yew staff in the ground, where it took root in the churchyard and is known as St Congar's Walking Stick.

③ On reaching the main road, turn

right and right again into **Kent Road**. Continue along **Kent Road** until this meets again with the A370 and turn right into **Wrington Lane**.

④ At the end of the lane, turn left and immediately right onto a drive to **The Woodlands**. In about 50 yards, fork left to follow

LOOKING BACK TO WRINGTON CHURCH

the signposted footpath leading to **Woolmers** and **Wrington Hill**. Ignore a gated entrance to woodland on your left and continue straight ahead to cross a stile and follow the obvious path as it enters the woodland.

Having reached **Woolmers** on your left, continue straight ahead, maintaining the same direction until, just before reaching a metalled road, it bears left.

⑤ Turn right at the road to proceed up **Wrington Hill**. Ignore the right

turn to **Bracken Hill** but, ¼ mile after this, turn right onto a signposted bridleway. This track is **Bullhouse Lane**, which you will follow all the way down to the village of **Wrington** (ignoring a track off to the right about ½ mile after leaving the road).

Turn left into **Roper's Lane** and in 50 yards, before **Yeoman's Orchard**, turn right onto a pathway which leads to the **High Street**. Turn left into the **High Street** to reach the **Plough Inn**.

Date walk completed:

Walk 18

CHEW VALLEY LAKE
AND CHEW MAGNA

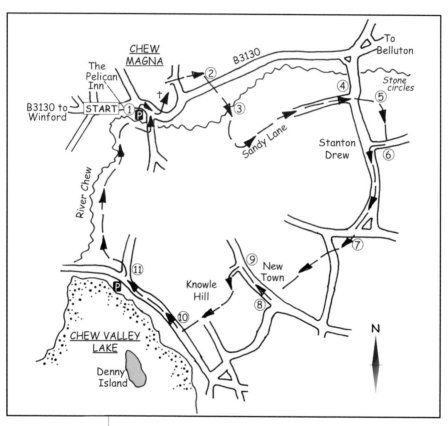

Distance:
6½ miles

Map: OS Explorer 155 Bristol & Bath, Keynsham & Marshfield

Starting Point:
The free car park
behind the Pelican
Inn in Chew
Magna.
GR 576630

How to get there: Chew Magna is on the B3130, which
runs between the A37 and A38 to the south of Bristol. The
Pelican inn is in the centre of the village. An alternative
starting point is the lakeside picnic area (pay & display
parking) at point 11 on the walk.

THE PELICAN AT CHEW MAGNA

*T*his interesting and enjoyable walk gives wonderful opportunities to appreciate both the history and natural history of the area, with three decent pubs along the way! The route passes the standing stones at Stanton Drew, older than Stonehenge, and returns via Chew Valley Lake, one of the best locations in the South West for wildfowl. Coots, tufted ducks, great crested grebes and many other waterfowl can be seen all year round, with other rare species such as pintail, shoveller, pochard, smew and many more adding to the list of regular sightings. Just off the route of the walk, a visit to Herriot's Bridge on the lakeside is a particularly popular spot for birdwatchers. When the manor of Chew was held by the Bishop of Bath and Wells (from 1062 to 1548), it was named Chew Episcopi or Bishop's Chew. It is now called Chew Magna and lies on the northern edge of the Mendip Hills. Its fine buildings, built on the wealth from its woollen industry, have resulted in Chew becoming a conservation area, allowing the village to maintain its charm. Fishing and tourism now provide an additional source of revenue, with the Chew Valley Lake providing excellent trout fishing.

The **Pelican** is conveniently right alongside the car park. It dates back to 1615 and the pub sign shows Sir Francis Drake's ship, the *Golden Hind*, which of course was originally called the *Pelican*. It is a traditional village pub serving home-cooked food and offering a small beer garden, which can be accessed from the car park. It's a friendly inn and boasts that 'The Pelican fits the Bill'!

Telephone: *01275 332448.*

Alternatives are the **Druid's Arms** at Stanton Drew (which has a large beer garden containing the famous standing stones) and the **Pony and Trap** at New Town.

The Walk

① From the car park, return to the main street. Just across to the right is the village church. Take the path into the churchyard. Keeping the church on your left-hand side, bear left to cross a bridge and then turn right. Follow **North Chew Terrace** to its end, ignoring the footbridge on your right. Continue ahead and cross the road junction to follow the signposted byway. Your path follows a high wall on the right. Follow this wall round to the right to reach the **B3130**.

The church is well worth a visit – don't miss the painted effigy of a knight wearing an interesting smile.

② Turn left and in 50 yards turn right into **Sandy Lane**, which is waymarked as part of the **Three Peaks Walk**.

③ Cross over the **River Chew** and then bear right to pass '**Paradise**' and its white cottage. The lane bears left and, on the bend, footpath signs tempt you to enter a field. Ignore these and just continue along the lane (**Sandy Lane**) until you reach the village of **Stanton Drew**.

④ Turn right at the Lecture Hall, where you will see the **Druid's Arms** just around the corner.

In the gardens of the Druid's Arms you can find the standing stones known as the Cove, dating back to around 2,500 BC, probably a Bronze Age ritualistic site. Access to the stones is permitted to patrons of the Druid's Arms. A small charge is made. The Cove consists of two standing stones with a recumbent slab between them. *The tallest is about 4½ metres high and, mineralogically, they are quite different in composition from other stone circles which you will soon be passing. There are three in the area, the largest being second only in size to that at Avebury.*

After retracing your steps from the inn, pass the Lecture Hall and keep straight on, turning right at **The Cottage** just after **Sandy Lane**. Keep to the right and, as you go round the corner, you will see the village church before you and a farm gate to your left, next to which a signpost points to the stone circles. Pass through the stile by the farm gate to proceed along the tarmac farm road towards the barns.

From here you can see the three stone circles creating a smaller version of Stonehenge. The Great Circle is by the River Chew and was originally of 30 stones. Local legend has it that in centuries past a midsummer wedding party continued on past midnight. The musicians were persuaded to play by the Devil. In the morning, the wedding party and the musicians were found transformed into stone. In 1997 archaeologists using magnetic field equipment discovered evidence of nine concentric circles of post holes. This proved the presence of an

enormous temple, twice the size of Stonehenge and dating back a further 500 years.

⑤ On reaching the second field gate, the road continues onward. Turn right here just before the gate, keeping the field boundary on your left. In a short distance cross a stile marked with a footpath sign, with a line of houses uphill before you. Continue towards the houses, keeping to the right of the field boundary, until you emerge onto the road alongside the junior school.

⑥ Turn right onto the road and then turn left at the T-junction, signposted to **Chelwood** and **Bath**. Follow this road, taking the right fork just after a telephone box.

⑦ On reaching the next road junction, head for the stile opposite, crossing this and veering to the right to cross to the next stile. Follow the path from here up into the wood. Enter the wood over the stile and follow the path through to reach a road. Go straight across at the road, following the footpath signs. Keep heading in the same direction across two fields, keeping the farm and the field boundary to your left, to reach a metalled road.

⑧ Turn right onto the road and shortly after the **Pony and Trap** inn, turn left onto a lane signposted **Knowle Hill**.

⑨ The lane winds around **Knowle Hill** on your right-hand side. Shortly after **Knowle House**, turn right to cross a cattle grid and courtyard. Go past the **Old Granary** and through a gate on your left. Turn right and head downhill, towards **Chew Valley Lake**. Cross a stile and continue towards the lake with a hedge on your right-hand side.

⑩ On reaching the road, turn right and in a few yards you enter a picnic area. From here follow the signs to the lakeshore. Turn right, cross the car park and, with the lake on your left, continue to yet another picnic site, this one with a tea shop and visitor centre.

Chew Valley Lake is one of the most important ornithological sites in the West of England. It is the fifth largest man-made lake in the country, built in 1950. The range of birds to be seen here is

DENNY ISLAND ON CHEW VALLEY LAKE PROVIDES A WILDLIFE HAVEN

dependent on the time of year and the level of water in the lake. Bitterns may over-winter here but are rare and very difficult to spot, being so well camouflaged. Amongst the winter visitors are the Bewick swan, shoveler, pintail, long-tailed duck, red-breasted merganser, goosander, smew, water rail, water pipit and many other rare species. So this is an attractive walk at any time of year, especially for those interested in the bird life around the lake. Herriot's Bridge is a good point from which to view the wildfowl.

⑪ Keeping the café on your left, walk up to the road. Across the road is **Denny Lane**. On the corner is a footpath sign next to a stile. Take this path and walk through the field parallel to **Denny Lane** until you reach a metalled path. Turn left here and before reaching the **River Chew** turn right to follow its course towards **Chew Magna**. Approaching the village, pass through a gate and, at a T-junction, turn right. When the lane splits, take the left-hand path to the main road. Turn left again at the T-junction with the main road. This leads you over the medieval **Tun Bridge** with its three pointed arches. You are now heading back up towards the church where the walk started. At the next junction, turn left to find the car park and the **Pelican** inn on your left.

Date walk completed:

PRISTON

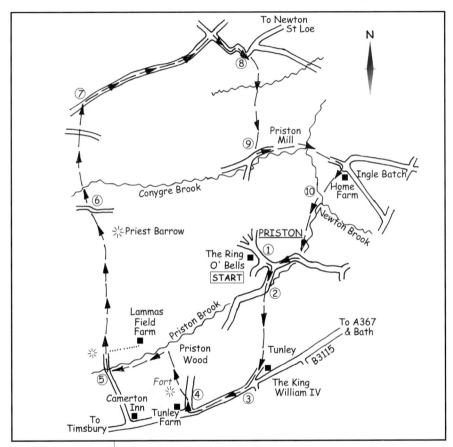

Distance:	**Map:** OS Explorer 155 Bristol, Bath, Keynsham and Marshfield
7 miles	

Starting Point:
Priston village
centre.
GR 694605

How to get there: *Priston is situated 4 miles south-west of Bath. From the B3115, which runs between Timsbury and the A367, turn north at Tunley Farm on the brow of the hill into Priston Lane, which is not signposted. In Priston village, turn left at the T-junction. The Ring O' Bells will be found on the left-hand side. Please park considerately on the streets in the village.*

THE RING O' BELLS AT PRISTON

*C*onveniently positioned for a day in the countryside from the cities of Bath and Bristol, this delightful walk through pleasant hill-country is somewhat unusual in that for much of the journey you will be 'beating the bounds' of the parish of Priston, with the route just making a few short detours. Since the parish was founded in Anglo-Saxon times, you follow a route that has been trodden for a thousand years. Priston is perhaps best known for Priston Mill, an ancient watermill which was once part of the monastic estate which in AD 931 King Athelston gave to Bath Abbey. It is part of the Duchy of Cornwall estate and, although once open to the public, is now a venue for weddings and similar events. The watermill and associated machinery are still operational. The village hall once served as the parish workhouse but was converted to use as a school in 1838. The area around Priston is hilly agricultural land and provides very pleasant walking.

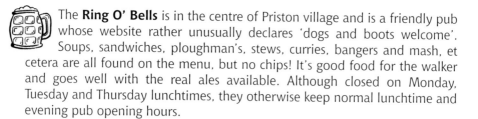

The **Ring O' Bells** is in the centre of Priston village and is a friendly pub whose website rather unusually declares 'dogs and boots welcome'. Soups, sandwiches, ploughman's, stews, curries, bangers and mash, et cetera are all found on the menu, but no chips! It's good food for the walker and goes well with the real ales available. Although closed on Monday, Tuesday and Thursday lunchtimes, they otherwise keep normal lunchtime and evening pub opening hours.

Telephone: *01761 471467.*

The **King William IV** at Tunley is close to the route and offers an alternative venue. This family-run 19th century coaching inn will be found on the B3115 and offers fresh-cooked food in a country setting. Accommodation is available, dogs are welcome and credit cards accepted.

Telephone: *01761 470408.*

The Walk

① From the **Ring O' Bells**, walk back to the T-junction where you turned left as you drove in. Turn right here, into **Priston Lane**, with **Hill View** on your right, to walk back along the road by which you entered the village. Follow the road downhill to the valley bottom.

② Where the path forks, turn left, heading towards **Rockhill House**, after which continue in the same direction as the road becomes a footpath. Continue uphill to a gate. Turn right just before the gate to follow the left-hand field boundary. Follow this path until, after it widens into a bridleway, it reaches the **B3115**.

③ Turn right onto the main road and continue for ½ mile to the brow of a hill. Here, just before **Tunley Farm**, turn right onto the road by which you previously entered the village.

④ In about 100 yards, immediately after a field gate, turn left to go over a stile.

To your left is the mound of an Iron Age hill fort.

Follow the left-hand field boundary until it bends sharp left and then right. Ignore the stile at this bend and continue in the same general direction, keeping to the left-hand

field boundary.
Your path now
leads downhill
with **Priston
Wood** to your
right and a smaller
wood to your left.
With the smaller
wood on your left,
you reach a gate.
Go through the
gate and continue
downhill to the
stream. Turn left
immediately
before the stream.
Keeping the stream
on your right-hand
side, continue until you reach a
metalled road.

PRISTON CHURCH

⑤ Turn right onto the road and
follow to its end at **Lammas Field
Cottage**.

*From here, you will be following
the parish boundary as it heads
north and then bears eastwards.*

At the cottage, cross the stile on
your left-hand side, turn right
and follow the right-hand field
boundary. Enter the next field and
again follow the right-hand field
boundary.

*As you enter the field, notice the
old sheep dip on your left and also
the small but prominent knoll on
the same side.*

Pass through the next gate to enter
another field and continue in the
same direction. You will see the
knoll of **Priest Barrow** ahead and
you will pass just to the left of
this. As you approach the barrow,
cross a stile in order to follow the
left-hand field boundary to reach a
metalled road.

⑥ You emerge onto the road just
where it does a double-bend.
Midway between the two bends,
pass through a field gate on your
right and follow the left-hand field
boundary. In about 200 yards, you
drop downhill to cross **Conygre
Brook**, using stepping stones.
Continue straight on, heading
uphill and to the left of a stand of
trees, to a metalled road. Go
straight across to follow a track

between hedgerows to reach another metalled road.

This track you have been following northwards is the old salt road and still forms part of the parish boundary.

⑦ Turn right onto the road and follow this for 1 mile to a crossroads. Turn right at the crossroads to head for **Wilmington**.

This section follows the parish boundary with Stanton Prior and includes a good uphill stretch. The views are worth taking in at the top.

⑧ Pass through the village of **Wilmington** until, immediately after **Stone Lea Cottage**, cross a wooden stile in a stone wall. From here follow the footpath south heading for **Priston**. After crossing a second stile, follow the path down into the valley. Keep to the right of the water trough to reach a stile at the bottom of the field. Use this to cross the brook and then head uphill to a point where a line of telegraph poles meets the hedge.

After crossing another stile, head straight across the next field to reach a gate from where you follow a well-defined track down to a metalled road.

⑨ Turn left and walk past **Priston Mill** to the end of the road. There is a choice of two footpaths before you. Take the one that goes straight ahead into a field, heading for the right-hand corner, to cross a footbridge where **Conygre** and **Newton brooks** converge. In a few yards, cross the stile on your right-hand side. A line of telegraph poles leads you to a corner of the next field and onto a farm track. Cross a stile on your right-hand side, just before **Home Farm**, and follow the white markers to cross another footbridge over **Newton Brook**, just to the right of where it converges with **Priston Brook**.

⑩ Continue straight ahead, keeping **Priston Brook** to your left, until you reach a metalled road. Turn right on the road to walk back to the village and the **Ring O' Bells**.

Date walk completed:

WELLOW

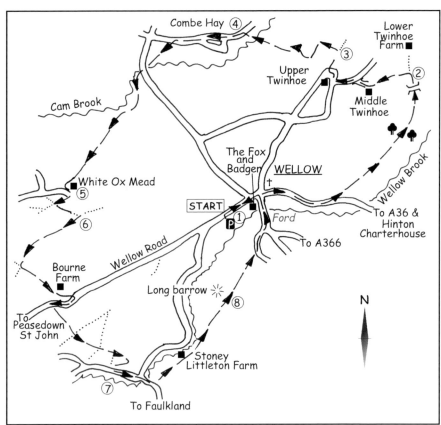

Combe Hay ④
Lower Twinhoe Farm ■
③
Upper Twinhoe ■
②
Middle Twinhoe ■
Cam Brook
The Fox and Badger / WELLOW †
Wellow Brook
White Ox Mead ■ ⑤
START
① P / Ford
To A36 & Hinton Charterhouse
⑥
To A366
Wellow Road
Bourne Farm ■
Long barrow ⑧
N
To Peasedown St John
Stoney Littleton Farm ■
⑦
To Faulkland

Distance:
8½ miles

Map: OS Explorer 142 Shepton Mallet and Mendip Hills East

Starting Point:
The public car park in the centre of Wellow, on the south side of the road to Peasedown St John.
GR 738582

How to get there: *From the A36 just south of Freshford, take the turning west, signposted Hinton Charterhouse and Wellow. At Hinton, go straight across at the crossroads and on into Wellow. Pass the church (right) and Fox and Badger (left) to reach the public car park on the left.*

THE FOX AND BADGER AT WELLOW

The Fox and Badger offers a welcoming atmosphere and meals to suit the family. Children are permitted in the restaurant area only. At the rear is a courtyard with tables and chairs. Well-behaved dogs are welcome. The pub is a free house and Butcombe's is the resident real ale, not having to travel too far from the brewery.

Telephone: *01225 832293.*

The **Wheatsheaf** in Combe Hay offers a suitable alternative. It is a fine looking building with terraced gardens. Dating back to 1576, it became an inn in the 18th century and with its wooden beams and log fire creates a wonderful atmosphere. Good food and real ales are on offer and again well-behaved dogs are welcome. Accommodation is also available.

Telephone: *01225 833504.*

So close to Bristol and Bath, yet right in the heart of the countryside, this walk begins at Wellow and loops around through the valleys and hillside of the surrounding area, passing through a number of farms. The highlight of the walk must be the Stoney Littleton Barrow, the interior of which can still be accessed – so bring a torch. One or two short stretches of the walk can suffer from nettles in the high season and suitable trousers are advised. Wellow has a long history and the area was extensively farmed even during the days of the Roman occupation. A substantial villa was found just to the west of the village. The south-facing slopes along parts of the walk could well have provided suitable vineyard sites.

 The Walk

① From the car park, head back towards the church.

The church at Wellow is well worth a visit, with its carved timber roofs and 15th century rood screen and frescoes. The village of Wellow is within the Cotswolds Area of Outstanding Natural Beauty and lies beneath Woodeboro Barrow. It is on an old tram road from the now disused coal mines at Welton to the Kennet and Avon Canal, and was once the proud possessor of a railway station on the old Somerset and Dorset line, which closed in 1966. The Wellow Brook runs through the village, and can boast a late medieval packhorse bridge. The brook rises in the south, near Radstock, famous once as a coal mining town, and flows

through Wellow on its way to join the Cam Brook at Midford. Both of these will be passed on this walk. The valley sides along the brook have occasional lines of trees indicating the presence of streams which result from the numerous springs in the valley.

Continue beyond the church to pass under a viaduct. Just after the **Wellow Trekking Centre**, follow the bridleway track which leads off to the left. When the track starts to become indistinct, cross to a hedge and continue above the hedge to a track that takes the bridleway into and through a wood before it drops down to the bottom of the valley.

Where a bridleway is signposted to the right, turn left to pass under the bridge of a disused railway line.

② With **Lower Twinhoe Farm** ahead of you, turn left onto a green lane to head uphill. As you reach the top of the hill, and a thistled area, the track once again becomes indistinct. Bear right and, keeping **Middle Twinhoe Farm** to your left, reach a gate. Turn right onto the farm road to reach a metalled lane. Turn left and then go round to the right of the farm buildings before bending round to the left again. Continue towards **Upper Twinhoe** but, just before the farm, turn right onto a signposted track leading downhill.

③ In about 150 yards, turn left through a double gate to follow the top edge of a field, keeping to the right-hand field boundary. Follow this track through the next field and continue along the track as it drops downhill through woodland to cross the **Cam Brook** and reach a metalled road.

④ Turn left onto the road and go through the village of **Combe Hay**, past the manor house. Just after the last house in the village, turn left through a gap in a wall where you bear right to drop down towards the **Cam Brook**, always keeping the brook on your left. On reaching the metalled road, cross the bridge and turn right to follow the Cam Brook again in the same direction, but this time with the brook on your right.

Pass through a field, a wood and another field to reach a stile. Continue ahead across the lower end of the field to a gate. Before the gate, turn left to follow the right-hand field boundary uphill to a stile on the right-hand side. Entering the next field, turn half-left to head for the top left corner of the field, where you enter a bowered track. At the top end of this, bear right to enter a lane and turn uphill to reach **White Ox Mead**.

⑤ In 50 yards, cross a stile and head for the next stile. Continue up a tarred track to where it splits at a shelter.

⑥ Above the shelter, turn right onto a narrow track. Continue for ½ mile, dropping gently downhill, until you reach a crossing of tracks. Turn left and follow the track down through **Bourne Farm** to reach the **Wellow Road**. Turn right on the road and continue downhill to **Double Hill Farm** at the bottom of the valley. Turn left into the farmyard to pass through a gate alongside a barn and enter a field, which appears to fulfil the role of a tractor graveyard.

Bear right to cross the stream and then follow the left-hand field boundaries through a series of fields as the track follows the stream. Eventually you reach a hedged trackway which crosses your path. This is **Brinscombe Lane**. Continue straight ahead, following the field boundary and stream as before, until the stream drops away to your right down through a paddock. Continue ahead to reach a track that crosses yours and here turn right to drop down to the metalled road.

⑦ Turn left on the road to drop down to the **Wellow Brook**. Cross the brook and continue ahead uphill. Turn left onto the track leading to **Stoney Littleton Farm**. Pass through the farmyard and through a gate into a field. In a short distance, bear left to drop down towards the **Wellow Brook**, where a footbridge crosses the brook. Do not cross the bridge but instead walk past it to cross a waymarked stile.

Follow the left-hand field boundary to cross the next stile, after which you turn left, signposted 'Stoney Littleton Barrow'.

⑧ At the next stile, turn right to walk to the top of the mound.

The barrow dates back 5,000 years to the New Stone Age. A stone entrance will be found at the southern end. At the time of writing, it was still possible to enter the barrow into a passage with burial chambers on either side. The site is now in the care of English Heritage. If entering burial chambers is 'your thing', then it would be a good idea to bring a torch on this walk!

From the entrance to the barrow, head uphill to a gap in the hedge to

THE FLOOD MEASURING POLE AT THE WELLOW FORD

pick up the previous track. Follow the track here by turning left and keeping to the hedgerow. Continue in the same direction across the following field to pass through a gate and onto a track beyond it. The track reaches a metalled lane where you turn left and follow the road as it crosses the **Wellow Brook** over a packhorse bridge and ford before climbing up into the village. At the crossroads in the village, turn left to head for the **Fox and Badger** and public car park.

Date walk completed: